EMPOWERING THE CU

THE CITIZEN IN PUBLIC SECTOR REFORM

IMI *informatio*
Sandyford, Dubl
Telephone 20785
email I
Inter

Published by:
Commonwealth Secretariat
Marlborough House
Pall Mall
London SW1Y 5HX
United Kingdom

May be purchased from
Publications Unit
Commonwealth Secretariat

Telephone: +44(0)20 7747 6342
Facsimile: +44(0)20 7839 9081

ISBN: 0 85092-649-1

Price: £12.00

Printed by Abacus Direct

EMPOWERING THE CUSTOMER

THE CITIZEN IN PUBLIC SECTOR REFORM

Managing the Public Service
Strategies for Improvement Series: No. 13

Victor Ayeni

Commonwealth Secretariat
2001

FOREWORD

A strong and achieving public service is a necessary condition for a competitively successful nation. The Management and Training Services Division (MTSD) of the Commonwealth Secretariat assists member governments to improve the performance of the public service through action-oriented advisory services, policy analysis and training. This assistance is supported by funds from the Commonwealth Fund for Technical Co-operation (CFTC).

Commonwealth co-operation in public administration is facilitated immeasurably by the strong similarities that exist between all Commonwealth countries in relation to the institutional landscape and the underlying principles and values of a neutral public service. In mapping current and emerging best practices in public service management, the Management and Training Services Division has been able to draw on the most determined, experienced and successful practitioners, managers and policy-makers across the Commonwealth. Their experiences are pointing the way to practical strategies for improvement.

The publication series, *Managing the Public Service: Strategies for Improvement*, provides the reader with access to the experiences and the success of elected and appointed officials from across the Commonwealth. The current title, *Empowering the Customer*, is a continuation of this series.

One of the key ideas in current public sector reforms and efforts at 'reinventing government' is that of redefining citizens as customers. Essentially, this requires that state institutions and public service providers conceive of their role in terms of meeting the needs and expectations of defined 'clients' or 'users' who can exercise influence similar to that of the customer of a typical business enterprise. To this end, various market-oriented measures, public-private partnerships and new performance management approaches have been introduced, in addition to traditional consumer protection mechanisms, to promote genuine empowerment of the customer.

This publication explores some of these recent strategies based on Commonwealth best practice. It presents, among other things, guidelines for developing clients' charters, setting appropriate standards for public services, and meeting the expecta-tions of the socially deprived. The public sector is of course remarkably different from business, and not easily amenable to the conditions of a perfect market environment. The publication also addresses some of the implications of this issue for the implementation of the new management theory. It provides 'hands-on' materials and policy ideas for governments, practitioners and experts.

The *Managing the Public Service* series complements other MTSD publications, particularly the *Public Service Country Profile* series, which provides a country-by-country analysis of current good practices and developments in public service management. Our aim is to provide practical guidance and to encourage critical evaluation. The *Public Service Country Profile* series sets out the where and the what in public service management. With the *Strategies for Improvement Series*, I believe we are providing the how.

Michael Gillibrand
Acting Director and Special Adviser
Management and Training Services Division

ACKNOWLEDGEMENTS

This publication is based on a number of activities which the Management and Training Services Division of the Commonwealth Secretariat has organised in the area since 1997. First, we would like to extend our gratitude to all the institutions that collaborated with us in putting those activities together, notably the Consumer Education and Research Centre, Ahmedabad, India; the Civil Service College, Singapore; Public Administration International, London, UK; and the Office of the Public Protector, Pretoria, South Africa. As usual, the Commonwealth Fund for Technical Co-operation provided generous funding.

The publication is mostly based on papers and case studies presented at the activities referred to but unfortunately space does not permit a complete list of our indebtedness in this regard. Suffice it to say, however, that in addition to the references provided at the end, the publication has drawn extensively on the background materials prepared by the following individuals for an international seminar held in Ahmedabad, India in 1999: Ms Alice Garg (Chapter III); Ms Gloria Craig (Chapter VI); Ms Christine Farnish (Chapter VII); Prof Robert Kerton (Chapter VIII); and Mr D S Ahluwalia (Chapter IX). We are grateful to them and to other experts and contributors who have participated in relevant Commonwealth Secretariat activities over the years.

Ms Maureen Ofili-Njaka, Ms Ayo Davies and Ms Anne Mike-Agbakoba helped at various stages with the editorial and secretarial work. Thanks are due to Ms Christabel Gurney who did the final typesetting. With his characteristic dedication, Mr Rupert Jones-Parry, the Commonwealth Secretariat's Publications Manager, made sure he 'plugged' every excuse that we might have made not to complete this work as planned. For this, he rightly deserves to enjoy the last place on our list of gratitude.

Victor O. Ayeni
Deputy Director
Commonwealth Secretariat, London

CONTENTS

I. INTRODUCTION

THINKING DIFFERENTLY

The concept 'customer' is at the core of recent approaches to the management of the public sector. The idea that citizens are also customers who must be served well runs through all contemporary public sector reforms and measures at 'reinventing government'. The decline in the resources available to the state, coupled with wide-spread concern about the performance of public administration, has not only opened up the inherent limitations of traditional ways of organising and producing public services but also given pressure to greater public demand for efficient, accountable and user-friendly management. As a result, state institutions and public sector service providers are now required to conceive their role in terms of meeting the needs and expectations of defined 'clients' or 'users' who, in turn, can exercise influence similar to that brought to bear by a customer in a typical business enterprise.

The popular adage 'the customer is king' is as true of the public service today as it is of business. A customer-based approach, according to Osborne and Gaebler in their well-known *Reinventing Government*, leads to a number of important improvements in the quality of public management. Among other things it:

- Forces service providers to be accountable;

- Depoliticises the decision of choosing among competing providers;

- Stimulates innovation;

- Gives choice to people between different kinds of services;

- Limits production waste as it forces the provider to match supply to demand;

- Empowers users to make choices, making them more committed customers;

- Creates greater opportunities for equity because it avoids the need for separate institutions for the rich and the poor, which in fact means that the latter are disadvantaged.

All these are consistent with the prevailing consumerism. Still, putting the customer at the centre of public administration constitutes a major paradigmatic shift in terms of theory as well as practice. Commonwealth experience confirms that many countries face an uphill task in trying to institutionalise new management ideas and practices, which foster a wide appreciation of the customer as the centre of public service production and delivery. The situation is not made any easier by the contentious philosophical issues that have attended these recent changes. Public administration, as we have known it, is changed fundamentally when the relationship between government and the ordinary citizen is transformed from one involving rights and obligations into a market-based arrangement whereby influence is allocated essentially according to the customer's economic power.

As a new dimension to the management of government, the customer concept certainly has the potential to improve the quality of services enjoyed by the ordinary individual. But its implementation is often not that straightforward. Worse, poorly understood and implemented, it could have a seriously deleterious impact on the process of governance. In fact, the whole idea of a customer in the public service situation has been attacked by scholars who essentially see it as part of the broader attempt to introduce business-like practices into government and as a systematic destruction of traditional public administration values. The values of representation, equality, welfare and justice, traditionally associated with administration in the state sector, are not always easily reconcilable with market-driven principles of efficiency, productivity and competition.

Change is ultimately about improving the quality of people's lives. It can be argued that the poor and less privileged tend to suffer the most in a situation of serious threat to traditional public service values. This is even more so in poor developing countries that have tended to depend on the state for the provision of most public services. Furthermore, critics have suggested that new business-like practices that have seen more and more services transferred or contracted out to the private and non-state sector have the potential to undermine public administration and cause ordinary individuals to lose faith in its capacity to effectively meet their needs. All these raise a much broader question.

Countries are increasingly under pressure to pay more respect to the rights of their citizens as defined by various international conventions and national legislation. The universal recognition that citizens have a right to development, which ensures their social and economic requirements in addition to other political and civil rights, is a case in point. However, the fact that new market-based management could seriously threaten the achievement of those same rights is an indication that the concept of customer is a potential limitation on good governance.

EMPOWERED CUSTOMER

Notwithstanding these apparent apprehensions, customer empowerment has emerged worldwide as an ineluctable management concept. No country serious about improving its system of governance and administration can ignore its prevailing influence. The pressure to find new and improved ways of managing the public sector in the face of ever-growing public cynicism remains strong and is certain to be so for a long time to come. But it goes without saying that the new idea of managing the public sector better is not just about recognising that the citizen is also a customer; it is about empowering that citizen to be a credible customer who is genuinely benefited by the process of the public sector. The empowered consumer is well informed, able to exercise his or her choice, and can effectively manage the different forces operating in the market place. It also implies an established administrative capacity to counter all the potential negative shortcomings of the concept as a management tool.

Taken together, customer empowerment presents public administration with a number of critical challenges. First is the fundamental objective of making market-based strategies work effectively in the public sector environment. Second is the need to ensure that the concept of customer does not marginalise the principle of citizenship as an essential feature of the modern state system. Third, while the need to introduce more business-like management ideas is inescapable, this must be implemented in a way that does not disadvantage the less privileged members of society. Fourth, customer empowerment must be integrated with and used to reinforce other aspects of change.

Fifth, the public service customer must feel invariably as empowered as their private sector counterpart – in other words, firmly in the driving seat of the service delivery process. Sixth, given that the public sector often provides very limited choice, the need to find appropriate customer empowering strategies cannot be over-emphasised. Seventh, even after the two preceding points are addressed, there remains the fact that the public service does not have a consistent way of providing all its services. Different approaches and methods are required for the different service users. Eighth, is the need to guarantee value for money for those who demand and pay for services. Ninth, is to ensure that business and private sector providers are accountable to their customers. This is an essential part of the regulatory role of the state which has become even more important with the increasing transference of hitherto state functions to the non-state sector.

The aim of this publication is to help policy-makers and managers better appreciate the issues involved in developing and implementing measures to maximise customer empowerment. We are here dealing not only with an apparently new management tool but a concept with deep philosophical importance, around which many other contemporary ideas revolve. Previous publication titles in this series have elucidated different dimensions of these recent developments in the management of the public sector in the Commonwealth and elsewhere. While all these issues are inevitably related, the present volume ventures further into the territory by focusing on the role of the customer as key to the new management thinking. It explores important recent strategies of customer empowerment based on Commonwealth best practice. It presents, among other things, guidelines for developing clients' charters, setting appropriate standards for public services, and meeting the expectations of the socially deprived. The public sector is, of course, remarkably different from business, and not easily amenable to the conditions of a perfect market environment. The publication addresses the implications of this issue for the implementation of the new management theory.

Undoubtedly, serious customer empowerment programmes have to be all-embracing. It is impossible to fully appreciate the thinking about citizens as customers of public services without coming to grips with the broader institutional and intellectual context of contemporary public sector reforms. By the same token, it is difficult to see how customers can be genuinely empowered in the absence of a culture of transparency and commitment to democratic values. A serious effort to create the necessary conducive environment to facilitate concomitant reforms in all aspects of government is inevitably a pre-condition for successful empowerment (see Box 1).

Over the last decade and a half, Commonwealth countries have implemented a combination of measures to ensure that the public management process genuinely advances the interest of the customer. Nearly all Commonwealth countries have instituted democratic government based on open and competitive elections, and those that have not done so risk losing their membership. Various decentralisation programmes, market-oriented initiatives including the privatisation of government services and enterprises, public-private partnerships and value for money methods, as well as new performance management approaches, have been implemented to complement traditional consumer protection mechanisms. Consumer protection and empowerment are areas where state and non-state actors are actively in collaboration, all the more so in that institutions in both sectors now freely borrow management ideas from each another. All these developments are inextricably linked and work together in making empowerment a reality. While one single strategy is insufficient, still the proper approach is not to try to implement all of them at the same time. Commonwealth best practice shows that countries are more likely to succeed with a more selective and methodical customer empowerment strategy, which obviously does not lose sight of the link with the wider reform context.

Box 1

ELEMENTS OF THE REFORM CONTEXT OF CUSTOMER EMPOWERMENT

(Based on the experience of New Zealand and the United Kingdom)

- Changing the relationship between Ministers and departmental heads (or chief executives) to make the latter more directly accountable to ministers for the production of agreed outputs and for the efficiency of their departments.

- Giving chief executives virtually complete discretion in the mix of inputs, including staffing, wages and salaries, and promotions, which they use to produce the agreed outputs.

- Eliminating rights of tenure, initially for chief executives and other senior officials, and subsequently for the entire civil service.

- Opening initially senior, and later all, positions in the civil service to outside competition.

- Making a clear distinction between those governmental activities involving the provision of goods and services to the public, those providing goods and services within government, and those concerned with policy advice.

- Separating the previous functions organisationally in different public-sector institutions.

- Distinguishing between policy goals or outcomes, for which Ministers are responsible, and the outputs which are supplied by government departments in order to achieve these outcomes.

- Defining, as unambiguously and quantitatively as possible, the outputs which are expected from government departments, and the incorporation of these definitions into formal contractual agreements to be used as the basis for evaluating the performance of the departments and the individuals within it.

- Establishing a clear link between achievement of output targets and rewards and penalties for staff.

- Establishing a system of financial accountability, based on accrual accounting of inputs and on output measures.

Source: R. Myers and R. Lacey in *International Review of Administrative Sciences,* No 3, 1996, pp. 331–50.

II. DEVELOPING CUSTOMER ORIENTATION

THE CONTINUING DEMAND FOR QUALITY

The last few years have seen rapid changes worldwide with interest focused on new management approaches given added momentum by growing expectations by the public for more information, quality and high standards of services. There has been a drive in nearly all countries to more willingly transfer management approaches traditionally associated with the private sector to the public sector. New technologies have opened up new possibilities for carrying out more novel operations and for communicating more widely. Societies everywhere have become more demanding and yet conscious of the need to address the situation of their less privileged members.

Despite moves in some countries to 'roll back' the state, government in developed and developing societies remains big business. With most citizens as its customers, the importance of ensuring effective service delivery approaches cannot be over-emphasised. In a typical day in the United Kingdom, 700,000 people visit their doctors; 90,000 people attend an out-patient clinic; 18,000 people make an emergency call to the police; 7 million pupils go to school or college. About 5 million people work in the public sector, millions depend on state welfare benefits and pensions – and the great majority of citizens contribute to central and local taxation.

In India, according to recent statistics, central government staff total 3.5 million. If the officials of State governments, quasi-governmental and local bodies who draw their salaries and allowances from the government are included, the total number of civil servants in India comes to about 20 million. The Indian state is the largest employer, largest buyer and largest seller of goods and services in the country. Similarly, the Indian railways employ 1.6 million people and operate over 11 thousand trains per day. The Indian Post Office is believed to be the largest postal network in the world with a total of 155,000 post offices, 89 per cent of which are located in villages.

The size and complexity of the business of government has in reality not diminished significantly in many countries. But it has been affected by widespread financial constraints that governments everywhere face. The well-known consequence of this is the unceasing pressure to cut back on public expenditure and optimise the efficient and effective use of existing resources through the adoption and implementation of new and innovative management approaches. The overriding feature of these is the introduction of market-based strategies patterned on the experience of the private sector. A recurring theme in this new public management is the conscious effort to improve customer-orientation predicated on a fundamental shift in government management philosophy and practice in favour of the ordinary person served. In essence, it is an acknowledgement of the fact that public services, like those provided by the private sector, are products to be tested against the needs of service-users and purchasers.

CITIZENS AS CUSTOMERS

The term 'customer' refers to the individual member of the public who is the recipient of public services. To be a customer implies choice in making a decision about the different options available in the market place; without this the customer is essentially at the mercy of the service provider. Unfortunately, public service 'customers' have little or no choice over the services provided to them. Customer empowerment initiatives are essential because the public service 'customer' often has so little choice. The fundamental aim of a people-orientated programme, therefore, is to instil into the public service the same 'customer first' attitude which drives the best private sector companies, so that the dictum 'serving the public' becomes truly the watchword of every public servant. Building on this point, such initiatives necessarily include the attitudinal and behavioural approach that is needed in the public service, rather than just a technical description of a new way of providing and receiving services (see Box 2).

The concept of a 'customer' refers to someone who need not be a member of a defined community but who operates in impersonal markets where the ability to pay for choices made, rather than obligations to social responsibilities and duties, is pivotal. 'Customer' implies an exchange relationship involving an essentially monetary transaction. Equally, it carries the connotation of 'someone who desires, and then chooses, buys and uses a commodity'. The underlying argument for its use in public administration is that the quality of public services can be improved by subjecting them to market forces. The market empowers the ordinary individual. By redefining the role of the ordinary individual in terms of a customer in a market place, he or she is empowered, the argument goes, to make a reasonable choice. Choice means more powers for the individual, which in turn limits the need for direct state action, the root of many of the crises that have plagued public administration in recent decades.

This notion of the customer contrasts the concept of 'citizen', at least in the sense in which public administration has traditionally understood it. A citizen is a member of a political community, which establishes a network of political relationships linking the individual with government and the state. This link involves a two-way relationship – in reality a complex matrix of rights and obligations. The view has been expressed that the focus on the customer fundamentally misses this important dimension of the modern state and the role of public administration. But several contributors to the emerging literature on service charters and customer empowerment have been quick to point out that reference to the consumer does not necessarily absolve the state from its accepted obligations to its citizens in the delivery of public services. However, the underlying issue that all efforts at empowerment must address is how to reconcile these seemingly conflicting theories about the place of the ordinary individual in the modern state.

The UK initiative called the 'Citizen's Charter' is a celebrated attempt to reorganise public administration around this customer focus and yet retain the traditional notion of citizenship. Thus, as Mr John Major, former British Prime Minister, explains in his foreword to the White Paper:

> *The Citizen's Charter is about giving more power to the citizen; but citizenship is about our responsibilities – for example, as parents or as neighbours – as well as our entitlements. The Citizen's Charter is not a recipe for more state action; it is a testament of our belief in people's right to be informed and choose for themselves.*

RECENT INITIATIVES

Concrete actions to promote consumer empowerment and customer-oriented governance have in the main involved one or more of the following measures:

- Giving citizens as customers a genuine choice in deciding what service provider to use through combinations of strategies, for example provision of payment vouchers, direct involvement in decision-making, and elimination of the monopoly situation of public service providers. Put differently, these initiatives ensure that the customer can 'exit' the service provision arrangement when he or she chooses.

- In contrast to the above, measures such as the establishment of complaint handling systems or reform of the judicial institution are intended to ensure that the customer can air his or her 'voice' when things go wrong. As we see below, sensitive service providers ensure that this is an important aspect of their service guarantee (see Box 3).

- Separation of the role of government into three distinct parts, namely provider, purchaser and regulator. These are then implemented as much as possible by separate and competing agencies.

- Reform of the mode of production and delivery of public services. For example, use of the traditional approach of direct public ownership in order to secure a strategic sector that needs to be accessible to all; privatisation to bring about greater efficiency and market competition; government regulation of private sector activities; imposition of value for money principles.

- The introduction of greater transparency in the functioning of government and public bodies, such as in procedures for various statutory approvals, allotment of land and property, systems of assessment and levy of taxation, award of work tenders, large orders for procurement of goods and services, delivery of civic services, identification of beneficiaries under various government schemes, etc.

- Strengthening of the oversight role of government over the private and non-state sector and, of course, institutions that oversee government's own work. The prevalence of liberal democratic principles has given added force to this development which has witnessed efforts not only to consolidate the work of traditional institutions such as Parliament and the state regulators but the huge popularisation of newer ones, such as the Ombudsman. Two-thirds of Commonwealth countries have now established a national ombudsman office, and in the rest of the world an average of one new state or non-state ombudsman office has come into existence bi-monthly since 1999. This development, as a recent survey by Christopher Hood and others (1999) points out, has also seen the number of so-called 'internal regulators' multiplied manyfold in the last decade.

- Consumer surveys. These have been around for some time but have become more frequent and widespread. As a way of encouraging response, organisations now commonly offer various incentives for return of completed questionnaires, for example participation in a raffle draw.

- Monitoring feedback and anecdotal evidence of telephonists, counter staff and others who deal directly with customers. This information is regularly reviewed by managers and staff and provides (as in Botswana) useful input for the work of departmental work improvement teams and quality circles.

- Establishment and/or strengthening of consumer protection agencies (see Chapters VII and VIII). Closely related to this is the adoption and implementation of international quality standards, notably ISO 9000. Since 1996 Malaysia has extended the implementation of these standards to its Civil Service (see Chapter IX).

9

Box 3

METHODS OF LISTENING TO THE VOICE OF THE CUSTOMER

- Customer Surveys;

- Customer Follow-up;

- Customer Contact;

- Customer Reports;

- Customer Councils (use of resident councils to stay in touch with their customers);

- Focus Groups (bringing customers together to discuss a product, service, or issue);

- Listed contacts for assistance (in telephone directories, Yellow Pages, etc.)

- Customer Interviews;

- Electronic Mail;

- Customer Service Training (for employees, etc.);

- Test-Marketing (to test new services to see if people like them before imposing them on everyone);

- Quality Guarantees;

- Inspectors;

- Ombudsmen (these have been referred to as the hygiene – or toothbrush – of organisations);

- Complaint Tracking Systems (that track responses to inquiries and complaints to improve response time);

- Customer Enquiry Helpline (via Service Centres)

- Telephone Hotline;

- Suggestion Boxes or Forms.

- Local Citizens' Advice Bureau

Adapted from: D. Osborne and T. Gaebler, *Reinventing Government* (1993), pp. 177–9

■ The institution of Service Charters along the lines proposed by consumer organisations and public bodies for all public organisations with a public interface, followed by the prescription of quality and standards for public services, wide publicity about them, and agreement of the agencies to submit to and act upon periodic independent scrutiny of performance against these standards. In South Africa, the initiative known as 'Batho Pele', which means 'People First', is predicated on the underlying principle that public servants have a duty to serve the government impartially and with integrity and honesty. An important part of that duty is to ensure that the services the government provides are delivered to the highest standards and in accordance with the government's wish to respond to the needs of all the people of South Africa.

- Adoption of Service Charters by privatised bodies and business establishments along the lines of the public sector.

- Strengthening the grievance redress machinery at all levels accompanied by close monitoring of delays, the punishment of the delinquent officials and steps to remove systemic causes of grievances.

- Judicial reform to promote the access of citizens to quick and inexpensive justice in various courts and the introduction of simple and speedy procedures for settling disputes. Many Commonwealth African countries have recently implemented various aspects of this reform.

- Involvement of citizen groups and consumer associations in providing information to the public on services, in the monitoring of quality and delay, as well as the distribution of various benefits under government schemes; and a close interaction of the media, citizens groups and local agencies in ensuring prompt and continuous attention to local problems.

- Moving from a patron-client relationship to one of fostering partnership with various stakeholders and civil society.

- Establishing more flexible ways of providing services based on up-to-date technology, which facilitates equal access to all. For example, access to people in remote areas could be better realised through the decentralisation of the service provision function to local structures, use of mobile units, one-stop shops which cater for several service needs at the same time, and via computer and modern information technology. Australia (Victoria), Malaysia and Singapore provide interesting good practices in this area.

- Training and sensitisation of service providers and customer-facing employees, such as post office counter staff, to the importance of and methods for promoting user-friendly services. Ghana has recently implemented such training under its public sector regeneration programme. Singapore ensures that service providers are an integral part of its work improvement plans. Lesotho, Malaysia and Uganda are other countries that have emphasised this initiative.

- Removal of the anonymity of public service providers through, for example, the use of name tags.

- Regular monitoring of the achievement of published performance targets and dissemination of the same to clients and to the public at large. This is now a standard feature of all institutions that have committed themselves to the service charter concept discussed later.

- Direct involvement and participation of users and public in decision-making and implementation. A notable dimension of this is in the United Kingdom with the increased involvement of laypersons and other stakeholders in areas hitherto regarded as the preserve of professional and technical people.

- People's Panel. The United Kingdom presents a good illustration of this. In 1998, the Service First Unit of the Cabinet Office commissioned MORI, the market research company, and Birmingham University's school of Public Policy to set up a panel of 5000 members of the public randomly selected from across the UK and representative of a cross-section of the population. Members are consulted on how public services can be delivered and how that delivery can be improved from the point of view of users. The panel provides a database of individuals that can be used for a wide range of research and consultation, to track attitudes and opinions over time and determine reasons for change.

- Incorporation of customer satisfaction standards in public service codes of conduct. Officials are obliged to maintain these and can be assessed by how well they do this. (See Appendix 1.) Granted that such customer satisfaction standards are often linked to service charters, this also provides an appropriate response to critics who underrate service charters because they are usually legally non-binding. Presumably, service standards could be enforced if they are part of a legally binding ethical code. Many Ombudsmen take the position that their role includes supervising the extent to which organisations have met their charter standards.

- Reform of the system of personnel assessment and appraisal to introduce more merit-based and objective measures that promote approved service standards.

- Related to the above initiative, but often applied to organisations rather than individuals, is the institution of quality awards (usually annually) for innovations and excellence in customer service. Quality awards are intended to induce competition and sharing of experiences between organisations. For example, the United Kingdom has an annual award under its citizen's charter programme (see Chapter IV). In 2001, South Africa instituted a 'National Award for Excellence in Consumer Protection', which is managed by the National Consumer Affairs Office (NCAO) of the Department of Trade and Industry. Although an inter-governmental professional association, the role of the Commonwealth Association for Public Administration and Management (CAPAM), through its annual Commonwealth-wide award for innovations in public sector management, also deserves mention.

- Implementation of Total Quality Management (TQM) as in Malaysia, Singapore and Jamaica, among others. Total quality is an all-embracing management principle, which 'focuses on the interactions of the external customer, external supplier, stockholders, society at large and the organisation itself, and specifically on the effective and efficient management of the processes which satisfies the need of the extended enterprise'.

■ Institutionalisation of freedom of information legislation to guarantee citizens and users responsible access to official information concerning government institutions. Australia, South Africa, Canada, New Zealand and India, among others, have built up significant good practices in this area.

III. EMPOWERING THE SOCIALLY DEPRIVED

THE SOCIALLY DEPRIVED AND VULNERABLE

A democratic government has the obligation to protect the interests of the weaker and more vulnerable sections of society, providing them, where necessary, with subsidised or free basic services and health care, and maintaining public amenities in the larger interest of the quality of life of the entire society. Socially deprived groups are probably the greatest users of public services and yet the least informed on consumer rights. These groups comprise children, women, the handicapped, elderly persons, the unemployed and those in the rural areas.

In developing countries, these groups form a large proportion of society. According to the 1991 census figures in India, the rural population accounts for about 75 per cent of the country's total population. The rural population is largely poor and uneducated. Taking advantage of these factors, producers and manufacturers generally dump substandard products on the rural market. It is not uncommon that products whose 'sell by' dates are close to expiry and goods that have been unsuccessful in the urban markets are supplied to them. Handling instructions on products are often not given in local languages and are, therefore, not understood by the people who buy them. Services such as a potable water supply, electricity, transportation and communications are not always available and, where available, are usually substandard.

In some countries, such as India, villages are located in remote areas with inadequate transport facilities. This causes difficulties in the regular supply of consumer goods. During health emergencies, these rural consumers cannot obtain proper and adequate treatment because of the lack of transport facilities. Students as consumers need adequate transportation for their education and exposure to the outside world. Added to these factors is the economic disparity between urban and rural incomes. Recent statistics in India showed rural per capita incomes as low as one-quarter of those in the urban sector, a difference of nearly 400 per cent. It is an established fact that income is directly related to the purchasing power of the consumer.

Yet many of these people actively participate in and support the existing socio-economic and political status quo that does not guarantee them the right to adequately take care of themselves. Unless there is effective independent regulation, which is hardly the case in many countries, there is the danger that rural people, and other socially deprived groups, will continue to be excluded or at best remain on the periphery of consumer benefits. The rapid growth of consumer protection organisations worldwide is, therefore, a welcome development for these groups. Unfortunately, in many cases the consumer movement has been essentially an urban middle-class phenomenon. This is especially so in developing countries where the needs and influence of urban residents easily overshadow those of the socially deprived groups.

MEETING THE NEEDS OF SOCIALLY DEPRIVED GROUPS

It can be argued that socially deprived groups are primarily concerned with basic needs necessary for survival – food, water, shelter, clothing, fuel, electricity, health care and education for their children. They are not, in the main, concerned with luxury consumer items. The issues which consumer organisations should, therefore, take up on their behalf are:

- The availability of essential materials;

- The provision of materials at low cost or as a social cost service;

- Ensuring that production goods are not harmful to the health of those who use them.

Consumer organisations should emphasise the need for adequate social cost services to meet these basic needs at the same time as working towards the goal of providing employment for all to ensure that the dependence does not become permanent. The Indian government has initiated a public distribution system policy for the supply of food grains to those living below the poverty line at half cost. However, this scheme faces implementation problems, for example about how to identify who is eligible.

It has been argued that the task of the consumer protection movement in respect of the socially deprived runs counter to the principle of trade liberalisation. But this is clearly incorrect because even industrialised countries with long-established free markets provide for these groups. The United Kingdom, for instance, has a high penetration rate of basic telephone access. Still, there are a small percentage of households who would like to have a telephone but cannot afford standard prices. The Office of Telecommunications (OFTEL) therefore requires British Telecom (BT), as the dominant operator, to offer special schemes to give these customers basic service levels at a lower price. One such package is 'Lifeline' which allows people to make outgoing emergency calls – to the police, ambulance, fire service – and to receive incoming calls. Another package allows people to make a small number of calls and, because this number is restricted, to receive a rebate off the fixed charge. There are procedures that allow customers who are in temporary payment difficulties to stay on the network but have outgoing calls blocked while they pay their bill in instalments.

OFTEL also requires BT to provide a service to everybody in the country, regardless of where they live, on the same terms. Thus, everyone can get connected whether they live in a remote rural area or in the centre of London. This is called geographic averaging of prices. Furthermore, OFTEL has special licence obligations for BT, requiring it to offer special services to disabled customers, for example, a text relay service for deaf people. To ensure wider public access, since 1996 the government of the United Kingdom has been implementing a plan to deliver at least 25 per cent of government services electronically by the end of 2002.

Box 4

QUICK AND EASY GUIDE TO MEETING THE NEEDS OF WOMEN CUSTOMERS

All government agencies have women customers. For some, women are not only part of the market, they are the market. Understanding and meeting the needs of women customers does not mean singling them out for separate help. It means, first, recognising where their interests and concern may be different from those of other customer groups, and then using this information in every aspect of an agency's strategic and operational planning.

Organisations that make women feel good and satisfy their needs will win their confidence and approval. Some questions that could be considered when planning and providing services for women customers are:

- What information is available from the agency's data base about women customers?
- What anecdotal information is available from staff who directly deal with them?
- Has any research being undertaken to identify women's needs, circumstances and perceptions?
- Are there services which seem to be under-used and, if so, what are the reasons?
- Is the format for community consultations such that women are enabled and encouraged to participate?
- What arrangements have been made to provide feedback to women participating in consultations?
- Is it appropriate to consult with women in other agencies, or non-governmental organisations, to add value to the decision making process?
- Is information about the programme or service included in media which are accessed by women?
- Do the language and visual presentation of publicity materials invite women's attention?
- Has the service been pilot-tested with women to gauge their response?
- Have evaluation procedures been established to enable data to be analysed by gender?
- Will the evaluation process assess the impact of services on women compared to other customer groups?

Source: Office of Women's Interest, Western Australian Government (1998)

GIVING VOICE TO THE VULNERABLE

The empowerment of deprived and vulnerable people inevitable means a secured voice in the stream of things. Giving 'voice' is not only to ensure that these groups of citizens and customers are provided with an opportunity to air their views about the services provided but also, and perhaps more important, to shift the balance of societal influence in their favour. As the perennial problem of electricity supply to Soweto in South Africa shows, people who consider themselves disadvantaged can become violent and unco-operative with authorities they think continually ignore their plight (Soweto has an unemployment rate of 40 per cent and many youths depend on pensioners' incomes for sustenance). In almost every case, such a development is an expensive option that could have been avoided in the first place. Giving 'voice' is inevitably an important first step to realising that.

In this respect, Commonwealth countries, like others, have increasingly paid attention to three crucial issues concerning less privileged customers. This of course is in addition to the fact that several of the initiatives mentioned in the last chapter have some implications for socially deprived people as well (see also Box 3). First, countries have tried to ensure that any institution set up to give voice to citizens makes special provisions for attending to the needs of those who are less fortunate or who need to reached through less conventional means. Many of such institutions have, in fact, committed themselves to relevant accountability targets. Some have gone a step further to specify such targets in their respective client charters. Ombudsmen of Banks, Social and Financial Institutions (commonly found in Commonwealth OECD countries) provide very interesting experiences of work to focus particular groups like the elderly, pensioners and women.

Second, Commonwealth countries have encouraged the establishment of specialised grievance-handling bodies for less privileged and disadvantaged people. Examples of such bodies are: Children's Ombudsman, Ethnic and Minority Ombudsman, Commission (or Ombudsman) for Women Affairs. While South Africa, and recently Sierra Leone, provide examples of these, both developed and developing member countries now commonly have one or more of them. Under a new plan announced February 2001 to reform the criminal system in the United Kingdom, the government proposes to establish an Ombudsman to champion the interests of victims of sexual assault (mostly women), child abuse and other serious crimes. There have also been calls recently in the United Kingdom for the appointment of a Disability Ombudsman similar to an earlier initiative. The recent emergence of so-called University Ombudsmen in Commonwealth countries (notably Australia and Canada), following the United States, is in many ways a realisation that students are an often-ignored special group with particular needs and concerns.

The third development is the increasingly widespread use of consultation as a tool of empowerment. Directly or indirectly, through non-governmental bodies and accredited representative groups, service providers and governments often consult with women, disabled people and other disadvantaged groups as part of their consumer survey programmes. All told, it must be said that many countries still have a long way to go in ensuring service delivery programmes that adequately cater for the needs of less privileged, deprived and vulnerable groups. The full extent of the importance of this issue is yet to appreciated in all countries. The existing institutional measures remain inadequate and sometimes poorly equipped. The cost of running specialised institutions, which could be substantial for many developing countries, does not make matters any easier. However, the evidence presented in this volume confirms that countries invariably have several possible approaches to choose from. For those that are determined to give voice to their more vulnerable and less privileged population, this fact could help to significantly mitigate the potential effects of the problems identified.

IV. CHARTERS AND SERVICE STANDARDS

WHAT IS A SERVICE CHARTER?

The service charter is also known by other names such as the citizen's charter, client charter, users' charter, etc. No less than 60 countries worldwide have adopted the idea, including all the developed Commonwealth countries and several developing members, notably South Africa, Ghana, Malaysia, Singapore, and Trinidad and Tobago. By whatever name it is called, the over-riding aim of the service charter is to shift attention to the customer in the context of a well-defined relationship with the service producer and provider.

A service charter is an important initiative to empower the consumer, whether as citizen, taxpayer or an ordinary service-user, and to promote and protect his/her rights in the market place of public service delivery and provision. Ultimately, it aims to re-order the accountability system by making public service providers directly accountable to their customers through assurance of quality, access to information and guarantee of redress when things go wrong. The citizen as customer is made pre-eminent (see Box 5).

Box 5

STRUCTURE OF SERVICE PROVISION
(United Kingdom)

Before	*Now and the Future*
Prime Minister	The Citizen as Customer
Chief Executives/Departmental Heads	Staff
Service Providers	Service Providers
Staff	Chief Executives/ Departmental Heads
The Citizen	Prime Minister

Simply defined, a service charter is a document which publishes service standards that customers are entitled to expect across an entire organisation or service area (see Box 6). It is a set of promises made to customers, but such promises must ordinarily be clear, meaningful and, as far as possible, measurable and auditable. They must also be sincere and seen to be so by customers and non-customers alike.

The service charter also includes statements on how customers can go about complaining and obtaining redress if the service they are given falls below published standards. The charter initiative focuses attention on desired outcomes rather than simply concentrating on the process. It is a product of consultation and consensus, involving customers, service providers and other stakeholders.

Although service charters define the rights and (sometimes) the obligations of customers in the service delivery process, they are in most cases legally non-binding. In this respect, they do not amount to a legal right, hence they are not comparable to a Bill of Rights or a legal contract between the service provider and its customers. There have been some criticisms of this position, especially that it confuses rights with expectations. As Bellamy and Greenaway (1995) have said about the UK experience, this situation 'undermines the citizen's right of redress and weakens the government's powers of implementation, making it especially dependent upon the goodwill of heads of agencies who may mouth the rhetoric of the Charter without ensuring that it is effectively adhered to'. This criticism has also been echoed strongly by observers in developing countries, notably India. These concerns notwithstanding, the popular position remains that 'legislative teeth' are not necessarily required to make the charter work effectively. After all, the aim is not to create a system to replace an existing one, neither is the intention to put officials and managers under unrealistic pressures. Legislative enforcement could also make the system inflexible and bureaucratic. Charters, in the main, define expectations, which does not guarantee that they will actually be achieved.

The emphasis of the service charter is very much on the individual and his or her relationship with public service providers. In theory, compliance is predicated on the fact that the individual invariably has the option of 'walking away' if his or her expectations are continually not met by the service provider. So, by implication, a credible service charter system needs a market that works well. But this, as we have pointed out, is not always feasible in the case of the public service. In fact, one of the purposes of charters is to help correct the weakness of the market. As William Waldegrave, the former British Minister for the Citizen's Charter (1991), put it, 'The Charter is a way of making sure that the pressures which would be brought to bear to the user's advantage in competitively provided services are also brought to bear on public services where little or no competition is available'.

Here we are faced with a dilemma: markets need charters, yet the latter cannot work well without the former. However, the solution to this problem can be found in the important emphasis placed in all charter systems on effective complaint handling mechanisms. With such a mechanism in place, customers are guaranteed a cheap and easy means of resolving differences they may have with the service provider. Furthermore, the position of the individual citizen could be made stronger through an elaboration of the standards offered by a charter. It should be possible to separate out standards that the service provider is able to guarantee from those that are

Box 6

PRINCIPLES OF SERVICE DELIVERY IN SOUTH AFRICA

The following principles apply to the delivery of all services to the public:

Consultation: Citizens as users and consumers of public services should be consulted about the level and quality of the services they receive and, wherever possible, they should be given a choice about the services that are offered.

Access: Every one should have equal access to the service to which he/she is entitled.

Service standards: Users and consumers of public services should be told what level and quality of service they will receive so that they are aware of what to expect.

Courtesy: Citizens and consumers of public services should be treated with courtesy and consideration.

Information: Users and consumers of public services should expect full and accurate information about the services they are entitled to receive.

Openness and transparency: The public should expect to be told how national departments and provincial administrations are run, how much they cost and who is in charge.

Responsiveness: Users and consumers of public services should expect that when the promised standard of service is not delivered, they will be offered an apology, a full explanation and a speedy and effective remedy, and that any complaint will produce a sympathetic, positive response.

Value for money: The public should expect that public services are provided as economically and efficiently as possible.

probably no more than 'statements of good intentions, which in fact may not be fulfilled'. This would certainly better clarify the customer's expectations and the grounds for insisting that they should be met through the available redress mechanisms. This enforcement process could even, as is the case in some OECD jurisdictions, allow for some form of monetary compensation. As pointed out in chapter II, the foregoing is reinforced in many Commonwealth countries by the work of the Ombudsman, practices such as awards for service excellence, 'name and shame' assessment policy and other strategies to mobilise the collective feelings of society. Equally, the inclusion of service standards in Codes of Conduct does provide some additional indirect means of judicial enforcement.

CHARTER THEMES AND DEVELOPMENT

Aspects of the key themes of a service charter are found in the *United Nations Guidelines for Consumer Protection*, an indication that the concept is not entirely new. However, the history of the service charter in its present form can be traced to the UK Citizen's Charter. This charter developed in the late 1980s from an initiative led by a number of local authorities in the UK.

Local government at the time was seeking to improve its accountability to the electorate and to demonstrate that it was delivering value for money services in the face of financial cutbacks. One way of achieving this was through the publication of quality of service standards for all the services for which a local authority was responsible, together with good complaint handling systems and redress if things went wrong. York City Council published the first Citizen's Charter in 1988. A number of other local councils followed and the Labour Party, then in opposition, began to express an interest in the idea of a Citizen's Charter for all public services.

In 1991, the then Prime Minister John Major surprised observers by personally taking up the Citizen's Charter as a key initiative of his government with the objective of improving standards in public services. He set up the charter as a 10-year programme. In the first half of its life cycle, the British Government published no less than 42 charters covering different areas of public service. For example, there is a Taxpayer's Charter which covers tax collection by the Inland Revenue; a Passenger's Charter for people travelling on British Rail; a Parents' Charter covering schools; a Patient's Charter covering doctors and hospital services, and a Council Tenant's Charter for people living in Council accommodation. In addition, there are over 10,000 local charters. All these charters guarantee standards of service that users of a particular type of service can expect across the UK. The government annually awards a number of Charter Marks to recognise excellence and innovation in the public service. The award is presented by the Prime Minister himself, not to the top managers but to the people who work in the organisation (see Chapter VI). Charter Marks can be withdrawn if an agency fails to maintain the level of service that won it the honour.

The service charter enables customers to check their expectations against what the service provider has offered. Since customers do not necessarily constitute a homogeneous group, it may sometimes be appropriate to formulate and publish separate service standards for the different groups of customers. The charter also offers the organisation a means to engage the customer on what it can realistically provide, bearing in mind available resources and the system under which they are allocated. Backed by a complaints handling system, it serves as a veritable feedback mechanism for management as well. To be effective, a charter must convey its message in simple, easy-to-read language and, preferably, in the style of a brochure publication.

Undoubtedly, the most important part of the charter is the 'Service Standards' or standards of service. In fact, this can be regarded as its very essence. According to the Treasury Board of Canada (1995), service standards 'are more than service delivery targets such as waiting times and hours of operation. They are about what people should expect of government, how services will be delivered, what services will cost and what clients can do when services they receive are not acceptable.' Standards relate to both outcomes and processes, and can be qualitative or quantitative. However, standards should provide a measure of the following features of the service, among other things: appropriateness; timeliness; consistency; accessibility; accuracy; and courtesy and sensitivity of provision.

The focus of a clients' charter is the external customer as against internal customers, who of course are no less important in the production process. The important point is that it is meant for distribution primarily to the external clients. Charters do not normally contain information about internal practices and standards of corporate services. In general, a typical charter comprises the following elements (see also Box 7 and Appendix 2):

■ A commitment to service – a pledge or set of principle describing the quality of service that should be expected;

23

- A description of products and services offered, and the benefits to which clients are entitled;

- Relevant legislation and legally enforceable rights arising from it;

- Identification of customers;

- Statement of guarantee for the level of service offered and delivery targets for key aspects of the service;

- Cost of delivering the service;

- A contact list, suggestions and complaints procedures.

IMPACT AND ACHIEVEMENTS

The potential impact of a service charter on public service delivery can be phenomenal. Concrete achievements of charter programmes in some countries of the Commonwealth provide a clue to these potential benefits which include:

- Establishing a new service culture in government and institutions;

- Serving as a planning tool by focusing on current expectations and future service needs at the same time;

- Ensuring that management and employees focus on people, not just systems;

- Providing a practical way of managing performance in an era of fiscal restraint;

- Encouraging the use of performance and customer satisfaction information to guide organisation operations and improvement;

- Promoting partnership between service providers and clients;

- Providing reliable means to measure service performance and cost, and a benchmark for performance evaluation;

- Within the organisation, it helping to define operational priorities and clarify workloads;

- Providing a veritable feedback mechanism for management, and thus information for future improvement;

- Improving public awareness of public service provisions;

- Organisations are encouraged to have clearer objectives, and staff a better understanding of what they are expected to achieve;

- Charter programmes benefit individual customers who are the recipients of services provided;

- Enhancing transparency and accountability while encouraging innovation and improvement;

- Ensuring that key principles are relevant and consistent with standard consumer protection principles;

- Information about government and its performance is more readily and widely available;

- Promoting people-oriented customer-sensitive governance;

- Encouraging the provision of vigorous complaint handling procedures;

- Presenting a new and better approach for enforcing public accountability that is consistent with prevailing management principles;

- Inexpensive to implement.

V. DEVELOPING AND IMPLEMENTING SERVICE CHARTERS

INTRODUCTION

The introduction of a customer- and people-orientated administration and the adoption of citizen's charters represent a paradigm shift in the way administration has hitherto functioned. Improving the public service process through charters entails, in reality, much more than the document in which the charter concepts are expressed. The former British Prime Minister John Major criticised a newspaper article for making the common mistake of equating the charter with the charter documents themselves. As he emphasised, 'it is far wider than that. The documents are only part of the story, one means to the common end of wider choice, higher standards and new ideas. This wider programme is about competition and choice. [The charter] is not a one-time job [but] a continuous process of setting, meeting and then raising standards over time.' This contention is equally evident in the initiatives of a number of Commonwealth countries, including Jamaica, South Africa and Australia. However, the charter should not, in the words of one British commentator, be reduced to an 'ever-expanding portmanteau team', lacking clear conceptual boundaries and taking on every new idea as it comes along.

KEY IMPLEMENTATION STEPS

The development and implementation of charters must be made against a proper appreciation of the extensive background preparation required for the initiative to be well grounded. There are a number of potential problems that must be guarded against. Experience also confirms that the process requires the sustained backing of key political and administrative leaders if it is to succeed. One other point that should certainly be emphasised is the need not to rigidly insist on uniformity, but to encourage local variations and sensitivity to sectoral peculiarities. The chartering process must be well managed and put under the charge of a responsible senior officer in the organisation. Taken together, an organisation proposing to adopt a charter is well advised to check the following implementation tips:

- Involve staff;

- Identify and review current services;

- Identify customer;

- Ensure that the charter is linked to the organisational planning;

- Develop service standards;

- Establish feedback mechanisms;
- Develop ways to handle feedback;
- Write, publish and promote the charter.

These tips can in turn be developed into a number of implementation steps. These should provide essential assistance in following through all the different stages that are required to achieve a successful programme. It should be said, however, that several Commonwealth countries have also published guidelines that could be used in conjunction with the following information.

Stage 1: Offer to adopt a charter programme

A charter programme necessarily begins with a deliberate decision to have one. Incidentally, the concept has increasingly become a standard part of Commonwealth administrative reform programmes. The decision to introduce service charters must ensure that:

- The idea is accepted as a legitimate creation of those concerned, and not seen as another foreign importation or imposition;
- It has the support of employees, together with top managers and the customers themselves;
- It takes into consideration the experiences of similar national and international institutions that have introduced service charters.

Stage 2: Planning and adoption

Some countries, like India and Jamaica, have appointed a special panel of experts and members of the public to advise on a suitable strategy and process for the introduction of the charter. In the United Kingdom, the Citizen's Charter was derived from a government white paper on the subject. Central Administrative Reform Departments or the Office of the Head of Government Administration can conveniently and effectively supervise the initial work leading to the adoption of a charter on the basis of an agreed strategic framework. Charters are most logically developed in the context of the organisational planning process so that the ensuing service standards reflect the organisation's strategic priorities and financial realities. While it is important that the programme is seen as a necessary part of ongoing changes in the administrative system, nevertheless its implementation has to be accorded adequate attention by ensuring that those responsible are not over-burdened with unrelated duties. Furthermore, extensive consultations with all relevant stakeholders must be seen as a valuable implementation tool at every stage.

Stage 3: Survey of the institutional environment

The service charter establishes a form of relationship between an organisation and its environment and it is, therefore, important that this is well understood. It can identify and review current services, and determine what may be expanded, curtailed or dropped altogether. Service providers must know who constitute their customers in the context of their core business. Information such as this may have been included in Stage 2. If not, it is essential that the subsequent stages to this are based on a well-informed assessment of the factors that are likely to influence the implementation and eventual impact of the charter programme.

Stage 4: Consultation and draft charter

This is probably the most important step so far, but the extent of what needs to be done will depend on the amount of work already done. Essentially, this stage entails:

- Consultation by the relevant implementation department with representatives of all stakeholders, including employees, top management customers and clients, interest groups and the general public.

- Agreement on service standards; duties of charts; mechanism of information dissemination and exchanges; grievance-handling procedures; and other relevant elements of service charters.

- Agreement on an appropriate administrative machinery for implementation, monitoring and review of the charter.

- The involvement of staff and provision of necessary training for the implementation of the initiative

- Undertaking research (in the form of customer survey, for example) to determine customer needs, priorities and services they value.

- Determining and establishing an appropriate feedback mechanism for receiving information on a continuous basis from customers and dealing with their complaints. As has already been pointed out, the system of complaints handling is of particular importance to the success of the charter. Drawing on the UK experience, a good complaints mechanism must be accessible and well publicised; simple to use and understand; speedy – establishing time limits for action and keeping complainants well informed of progress; fair; able to protect the confidentiality of complainants and staff; informative about the work of the organisation. It should also provide effective and appropriate redress.

- Agreement on dates and methodology of publication and effectuation of the charter.

- Establishment of some indication of the range of charter initiatives that institutions should encourage, and the extent to which departments and sub-units should be involved or permitted to pursue their own independent initiatives.

Box 8

THE SERVICE CHARTER IN INDIA – AN ASSESSMENT

The initiative of government toward citizen orientation of administration is a welcome step. However, a close look at the rhetoric and prospects of the existing charters suggests that these are a set of statements of good intentions not accompanied by the in-built mechanism necessary to achieve them. The empirical evidence reveals that even after two years of existence the citizen's charters have made no impression on the quality and delivery of public services, as most of the charters have simply remained on paper and have not reached the doorsteps of the citizens. Out of 79 citizens interviewed only 33 (42 per cent), were aware of citizen's charters. There are certain inherent weaknesses in India's citizen's charter programmes, which are likely to make them ineffective.

Firstly, the citizen's charters are not made widely available to the users of the service. Out of 33 respondents who were aware of the citizen's charters, only one succeeded in getting a copy. Through informal interviews it has been found that the managers of public organisations have not been marketing the idea of citizen's charters because of fear of mounting public pressure to improve the quality and delivery of public services. Out of nine organisations visited, only two had a copy of the respective citizen's charter. The remaining organisations have not received copies of their charters from the respective headquarters. In a case where the charters have been received by the zonal, divisional and branch offices, the middle and front line staff have not even read them. And none of the policyholders and agents interviewed had seen a full copy of the charter.

Secondly, although departments have issued a number of orders and specific guidelines for improving the standards of services, copies of these amended documents have not been made available to users. Thirdly, standards of service have not been explicitly defined. Fourthly, the rewards and penalties vis-à-vis announced standards have not been incorporated in the charters. Fifthly, the lack of an effective complaints machinery, which receives and disposes of complaints about quality standards is a major stumbling block in the acceptability of these charters to citizens. The rhetoric of redress of public grievances is at variance with reality. Mere setting up of the machinery for the redress of public grievances is not sufficient. Display of information about the grievance redress machinery, the name of the functionary/contact person and timings and place of his/her availability, courteous behaviour of the officials, and time limits for the redress of grievances are some of the important factors which determine the effectiveness of the machinery set up for the purpose. Sixthly, the monopoly of public service providers exerts no pressure on public organisations to improve quality of service.

Adapted from: B.S. Ghuman in *African Administrative Studies*, No. 55, 2000, pp. 17–27.

Stage 5: Implementation, monitoring and review

Ultimately, the implementation of the service charter is the responsibility of all since it recognises that employees and other stakeholders have different roles to play. However, it is the service provider with whom the customer is directly in contact who probably has the most important role in observing and maintaining the agreed standards. The charter is effected once its contents are agreed upon by all parties and duly published. The publication of the document and its content is therefore a critical stage in implementation (see Appendix 2). This needs to be properly managed and well-resourced as an on-going process. Published charters must be made widely and easily available.

PROBLEMS TO WATCH

It should be stressed that the clients' charter is not a panacea for all service delivery problems in the public sector. Service standards are only one aspects of what is required to make good administration a reality. Even more crucial, perhaps, is the issue of implementation. Implementing charters and ensuring that providers and clients abide by them is not a straightforward issue, as the experience of many Commonwealth countries confirm (see Box 8). Aspects of the charter system, such as the complaints handling process, could become an unnecessary drag on the smooth functioning of the organisation. Equally, there have been reports of attempts to manipulate records of achievements of charter targets. All told, it is fair to say that charter initiatives tend to be more effective when developed and implemented as part of a broader programme of change. Charters must be clearly linked to organisational planning, and used to clarify and promote the priorities agreed with users and clients. Establishing and maintaining service standards must be a continuous experience. Hence, a system of monitoring and keeping track of clients' expectations in order to ensure appropriate adjustments in service delivery must be an integral part of every charter programme. As one Commonwealth document emphasises, 'knowing where clients stand and how they feel about quality services should be a key priority'.

All told, the main problems usually faced by countries in implementing charter programmes can be summarised as follows:

■ Limited emphasis on customers' responsibilities;

■ Setting standards that are hard to monitor or, conversely, place too much emphasis on quantitative measures;

■ Offer exaggerated expectations;

■ Published charter not readily available or inaccessible to customers and employees;

■ Limited appreciation of the organisation's core business and who the customers are, leading to inappropriate standards or standards which are not consistent across the organisation;

- Not rigorous enough to ensure continuous improvement;
- People having limited awareness of their rights;
- The initiative not being 'owned' fully throughout the public service;
- The distortion of priorities by standards and league tables;
- The way in which improvements can be very gradual and not readily obvious;
- Rigid uniformity – instead, encourage local and service variations;
- Loose and obscure language;
- Wavering commitment and support at all levels;
- Lack of clear conceptual boundaries;
- Under-estimating the extensive background work required to introduce and implement the concept;
- Lack of continuity;
- Ignoring peculiarities of disadvantaged and vulnerable customers, such as people with disabilities and the elderly;
- Disconnection from a wider public sector reform programme.

VI. THE SERVICE CHARTER IN PRACTICE

BACKGROUND

The following case study is based on the United Kingdom service charter experience, known officially as the Citizen's Charter. The challenge of improving public services led the then British Prime Minister John Major to establish the Citizen's Charter programme in 1991. His aim was 'to shift the balance of change in society more radically than ever before into the hands of ordinary people'. The Charter was set up as a 10-year programme. It passed its halfway point in 1996 and this provided a good opportunity to take stock of what had been achieved and to look ahead to the second half of the programme.

THE CHARTER IN OPERATION SINCE 1991

Everyone uses public services, and most citizens use them every day. On a typical day in the UK 700,000 people visit their doctor; 90,000 people attend an out-patient clinic; 18,000 people make an emergency call to the police; 7 million pupils go to school or college; and 5 million people work in the public sector. The Charter covers these and many other public services. It applies to:

- All central government services, such as employment offices;

- All local authority services (the provision of housing, the granting of planning permission, the collection of rubbish);

- The health service;

- The education service;

- The police and fire brigades;

- Where relevant, to the privatised utilities such as British Gas, and the water and electricity companies.

The Charter applies wherever effective competition or choice for the individual consumer is lacking and it is based on the belief that all taxpayers have the right to expect high-quality public services that meet their needs. The Charter was set up on the basis of six key principles underlying public service. These are:

- Standards

- Information and openness

- Choice and consultation

- Courtesy and helpfulness
- Putting things right
- Value for money.

Standards: These are at the core of the charter programme. For each service, explicit standards are set which individual users can expect to receive. These are then monitored and the results published. For example, the Patient's Charter sets out that the customer should be given a personal appointment at a hospital out-patient clinic and be seen within half an hour of the arranged time. The Post Office Charter says that the customer should wait less than five minutes to be served in a post office, and that the Royal Mail should deliver 92 per cent of first-class letters on the next working day after posting. Rail passengers in 1992 were told for the first time the targets for the punctuality and reliability of trains.

Information and openness: The second principle is that full and accurate information should be readily available in plain language about how public services are run, what they cost, how well they perform and who is in charge. The Plain English crystal mark – a mark that the document is simple to read – appears on some 750 public service publications. There are plans to have it appear on all new and revised charters. Plans are also underway to improve the clarity of government forms by testing all new ones on users first.

Under the Citizen's Charter, public services now publish statistical information on the performance of individual schools, hospitals, police forces and local authorities. Now, parents can see how their children's schools rate against others in examination results and truancy levels. Local hospitals can be compared with others in key areas, like waiting times for general surgery. One can find out about performance on everything – from how quickly the police respond to 999 calls to the time it takes to process a planning application. To encourage this process, the Charter Unit in 1997 produced a CD-ROM which put together all the published performance indicators, to make them easier to use.

Choice and consultation: A third key principle is that the public sector should provide choice wherever practicable. There should be regular and systematic consultation with those who use the service. Most public services now consult their users both to gauge customer satisfaction and to identify areas of service delivery that are a priority. A range of mechanisms is used: surveys, focus groups, comment cards, etc. (see Chapter II). Such consultation leads to better service. It also helps to give power back to the individual. In social housing, for instance, it is now a requirement that a tenant should be consulted on matters that affect his or her house, and be given information on the way the local authority runs the estate. Furthermore, new freedoms have been introduced. Fifteen years ago, the local authority told people what colour they could paint their doors and it was generally a uniform public service drab green. Now people can paint their doors any colour they like.

Courtesy and helpfulness: This can range from public servants giving their names on the phone to changing opening hours to suit customers' convenience. Customers recognise the frustration of being passed from one anonymous department to another when they telephone a large organisation. As a way of eliminating this frustration, a number of services have set up one-stop points that enable users to carry out all transactions through a single point of call. Another innovation is that new mobile tax enquiry centres are placed on the High Street to help the customer. 'We are making it easier for you to pay your taxes' may not be the most eloquent election platform, but it is part of the change of culture that the charter has helped to bring about. Public services now aim to put people first.

Closely related to the principle of courtesy and helpfulness is the principle of fairness. The Charter stipulates that services must be available equally to all who are entitled to them.

Putting things right: Things can and do go wrong. But the public service should not be afraid of complaints, and managers should not try to sweep them under the carpet. The best private sector companies welcome complaints as an excellent means of getting feedback in order to improve service. In 1993, a task force was set up to produce a good practice guide on how to handle complaints in the public service. There is now an established independent route of complaint for all the major services and, where appropriate, compensation. This process has yielded results. For example, from information gathered from their local offices, the Central Employment Service puts together a report covering complaint statistics, issues of common concern and examples of improvement made as a result. In this way, both national and local units benefit.

Value for money: The last key principle is value for money – the efficient and economic delivery of public services within the resources that the nation can afford. This principle has given rise to many innovations. One of these is the redesigning of tax forms and leaflets to make them clear and easy to read. This, in turn, translates into financial savings for the taxpayer: because fewer people complete the forms incorrectly, fewer Inland Revenue staff are tied down correcting them. In addition, the Inland Revenue has colour-coded its leaflets to help people pick the right one for a particular enquiry. All of these have made things easier for the customer, as well as saved the public service money.

WHAT HAS THE CHARTER ACHIEVED?

An assessment of the first half of the 10-year charter programme shows up more positive than negative results. Awareness of public services has improved. Performance tables have proved a very popular way of showing people how their local services are performing. Research by the independent Audit Commission shows that eight out of ten people think this sort of information should be available. But the key point is that the information given to users is also an invaluable tool for managers. The introduction of performance tables for schools, hospitals, local authorities and police forces has allowed managers to compare their performance with those of others. League tables provide an incentive to action. No one wants to be at the bottom and there is a great incentive to improve.

At the same time, the very setting of standards focuses minds on the objectives of an organisation. It also enables managers to ratchet up standards every year in order to improve performance. The railways have over the last five years been able to increase standards for both punctuality and reliability. The result is better service for the passenger. Similarly the targets of London buses running on time has been raised.

But the benefits are not confined to the centre. At the local level, staff have the scope to do a better job. They have clear objectives and are responsible for meeting them, and so are able to be more responsive to the needs of the customer. At the same time, the charter programme enables government to recognise good delivery of public services. In 1993, the Charter Mark Award Scheme, an award for excellence for the public service was introduced. It is run on an annual basis and over the last four years some 700 organisations have won a Charter Mark, and nearly 3,000 organisations have tested themselves against it. The Award is presented each year by the Prime Minister, not to the top managers but to the people who work in the organisation. It is his opportunity to thank them for their hard work, integrity and professionalism. Over the past few years, the scope has been broadened so that users now nominate to the central Charter Unit those organisations which they believe deserve an award. Applications are subject to a rigorous assessment process. It is, therefore, not surprising that those who win a Charter Mark appreciate the official recognition of their performance.

But it is the impact on the individual citizen that is the key to the programme. The charter is raising standards and delivering real benefits to people. Examples of these achievements are given below:

- In 1991, there were 172,000 patients waiting over a year for hospital operations. By 1995 the figure had fallen to 4,600.

- It used to take up to 95 working days to process passport applications. Now, it takes a maximum of 15 days.

- 6.7 per cent more 16-year-olds now get five or more examination passes than in the four years prior to this period.

More importantly, public services now put people first and do not expect them to conform to the convenience of the organisation. Before the charter, it was not uncommon for block bookings to be made for hospital out-patients. Several patients were given the same appointment time and were expected to wait without complaining for long periods, and then to be grateful for being seen at all. Now, everyone gets a timed appointment and they do not have to wait for more than 30 minutes. An increasing number of out-patient clinics are open on Saturday mornings or weekday evenings in recognition of the time that is usually more convenient for patients. Many Benefit Offices, Job Centres and other government offices have changed their opening hours to suit the customer. Indeed, there is a fundamental change of culture taking place in the public service with the needs of the customer being increasingly met. This has made a real and practical difference to the lives of people at every level.

The Charter has undoubtedly raised public expectations. But this has also led to criticisms that government has promised more than it can deliver – a not uncommon failing for governments. The need to achieve set standards has put additional strain on those delivering services, particularly in areas like the health service where demand is on an inexorable upward curve. There is also evidence that, despite government efforts, many people, particularly those most disadvantaged, do not know their rights or are unable to exercise them. There has also been concern that the standards chosen and the demands of league tables can distort priorities. Furthermore, many of the changes achieved are in themselves small and local. This has meant that it has proved difficult to explain the benefits of the Charter to an often sceptical national audience. Criticisms need to be taken seriously. But overall, the picture is positive and a real change of culture is being achieved.

FUTURE PLANS FOR THE CHARTER

Localisation: When the Charter was set up, standards were agreed at a national level. There are now no less than 45 such national charters. But national charters are only a start. Local service providers are developing and improving on the national standards in their own local charters. In this way, charters can reflect local circumstances, needs and user views. There are already some 10,000 local charters covering individual doctors' surgeries, schools, social security offices, local authority services and hospitals. The goal is to transfer power from the hub to the spokes of the wheel so that better services are delivered on the ground.

Standards: The 1997 White Paper on the charter set down new central government standards, dealing with such things as answering letters, appointment times and consulting users.

Information: The Charter Unit has developed the CD-ROM that proved successful in 1997 with even more information on it. This information has been posted on the Internet. Cross-sectoral charters are being produced that will give people in certain age groups more information about their rights and where to go for help. There are also plans for new performance indicators, the most significant of which will be clinical indicators, showing how well hospitals actually perform in treating the customer.

Rights and responsibilities: There is the need to recognise that users' rights should be balanced by their responsibilities. Already there are signs that this is happening at the local level. Many schools have drawn up home/school partnership agreements whereby, for example, parents commit themselves to making sure that their children do their homework. A similar approach is being taken in the health service with a campaign to ask patients to behave responsibly: to tell their hospital as soon as they know they cannot keep an appointment; to call the doctor out at night only if they cannot wait until the next day; to dial for an emergency service only when truly necessary. These changes are not meant to impose new requirements on citizens but to provide information to people to encourage them to behave responsibly.

User involvement: As a way of encouraging greater user involvement, charters are being issued first in draft form, so that users and service providers have the opportunity to comment on the standards and targets. This is to ensure that the charter properly reflects their interests and needs, rather than simply being imposed from above.

VII. CONSUMER PROTECTION INSTITUTIONS AND STRATEGIES

INTRODUCTION

The discussions so far have focused essentially on measures that primarily target the public sector. In this chapter and subsequent ones, we look at those consumer protection measures that have traditionally been targeted at private and business sector production processes. As we have noted, these are no less important in today's public sector environment, and in any event the state has an important responsibility to ensure that all aspects of production and service delivery are effectively regulated in the interest of the ordinary individual. In addition to the regulatory role of the state, many non-state actors play a very active role in protecting business and private sector consumers.

The unfinished course of economic reforms and the requirements for participatory governance demand that democratic governments at all levels should be more caring and responsive to the needs of their citizens, not only in direct relation to the public service but also in the context of the wider economic market. In the neo-global order under a free market economy, the need for strong consumer protection mechanisms is of paramount importance. A common error in the rush to liberalise markets has been the assumption that the environmental framework developed over time in industrialised countries is readily available elsewhere. The market in itself provides a form of consumer protection by freeing consumers, for example, from monopoly control. But historical evidence shows very clearly that an institutional framework for fair market exchange is crucial for consumer welfare. This is especially true for developing countries that have only recently entered the market era.

Alfred Marshall, renowned expositor of the market economy, who wrote in 1892, captures their vulnerability: 'A race of wolves thrives [because wolves] ... are best fitted to utilise the environment for their own purposes'. In other words, there are sellers who thrive on the dark side of the market place. In wealthier countries, their growth rate has been reduced by established institutions which ensure fair market exchanges. But in less wealthy countries, where such institutions are absent or inadequate, they thrive. The market economy does not automatically create its own optimal institutions. Consumer protection institutions have to be painstakingly put in place and this involves a multi-dimensional approach.

LEGISLATION

The first point is legislation through consumer protection laws, competition and anti-monopoly laws, freedom of information laws, laws against discrimination, environmental protection laws, trade practice laws, including laws against misleading advertising, all of which should cover the public and private sector. It is universally recognised that the consumer has a right:

- To know

- To be correctly informed

- To be heard

- To free choice

- To safety.

In the main, the *United Nations Guidelines for Consumer Protection*, as well as the *United Nations Guidelines for Business Practices* provide the most promising models for enacting consumer-related laws. In many countries, the rights of the consumer are enshrined in the various forms of Consumer Protection Acts that exist. While North America and Europe have adequate consumer protection laws, the same cannot be said for a number of other countries, especially in the developing regions. In Ghana, efforts are being made to enact a law on consumer protection and towards this end model laws on consumer protection are being studied. A Model Law for Africa, drafted along the lines of the *United Nations Guidelines on Consumer Protection 1985* and the *Extensions of the United Nations Guidelines on Consumer Protection 1995* have been circulated to relevant institutions like the Ghana National Chamber of Commerce, the Consumer Protection Association and some private institutions for their reaction and input.

South Africa adheres to and implements the *United Nations Guidelines for Consumer Protection*. In Malaysia, a comprehensive Consumer Protection Act is yet to be introduced. However, there are 29 pieces of legislation with inherent elements of consumer protection, which various ministries and agencies administer. These include the Price Control Act 1946, the Control of Supplies Act 1961, the Hire Purchase Act 1967, Weights and Measures Act 1972, Trade Description Act 1972 and the Direct Sales Act 1993. Other laws that protect consumers in the market place are the Food Act 1983, Standards and Industrial Research Institute of Malaysia (Incorporation) Act 1974, Environmental Quality Act 1974 and Medicines (Advertisement and Sales) Act 1972.

Many existing laws are, however, inadequate to protect the rights of consumers, especially in light of the activities of powerful interest groups working to create an environment that permits the wolf to thrive. The Drug Control Ordinance of Bangladesh illustrates this point. When the policy was enacted, drug companies were initially compliant but they soon influenced politicians and bureaucrats to change the law in their favour. In Seychelles, although there are existing laws to control all imported goods, which make up 85 per cent of the country's essential commodities, suppliers often take advantage of uninformed and illiterate consumers. This situation is aggravated by there not being enough competition in the market place, with the result that consumers have limited choices.

CONSUMER ORGANISATIONS

Legislation alone may be insufficient to protect consumers and can only be a starting point. The formation of both governmental and non-governmental organisations with a watchdog role is necessary to enforce consumer-related laws, especially in areas where there is a monopoly of the market. Some characteristics have been identified as necessary for consumer organisations to be truly effective. They need to:

- Have a clear mandate;

- Have a power base;

- Have adequate resources;

- Have perennial resources (resources should be unconditional and the organisations must be able to generate resources at its will rather than depend on others);

- Be apolitical;

- Have the ability to provide redress.

The various types of consumer protection organisations that are found in Commonwealth countries all have similar goals:

- To give advice to consumers on their problems in the market place;

- To guide and educate consumers;

- To receive complaints from consumers against traders and intervene to get redress;

- To enforce consumer-related laws.

Differences in mandates and implementation vary according to the nature of the organisation and the peculiar situation of the individual countries. Thus in Solomon Islands, the mandate of the Consumer Affairs Division established under the Ministry of Commerce, Industries and Employment in 1988 includes the formulation of a consumer protection law and advising the government on how to enforce such a law effectively. The Division also establishes certain standards of conduct for those engaged in the production, sales and distribution of goods and services. In the UK, the role of the Office of Telecommunications (OFTEL), a non-ministerial government organisation to regulate the telecommunications sector, includes enforcing and modifying licence conditions.

In Sierra Leone, the Consumer Protection Council, a non-governmental organisation, was established in 1986 against the background of the Structural Adjustment Programme that required the country to liberalise trade. A subsequent survey showed that most items including the country's staple food were imported and this at high cost. As part of its functions, the Council began providing food grains and agricultural tools to farmers for food production. This resulted in the achievement of some level of food sufficiency, especially in war-affected areas. The Council also embarked on plans for extensive mechanised farming and the setting up of a micro-industry for processing locally produced crops. The escalation of prices of imported products was blamed largely on the scarcity of foreign exchange. The Council successfully advocated the introduction of foreign exchange bureaux which led to the stabilisation of prices.

The commitment of the Malaysian government to consumer welfare was reinforced by the setting up of the Ministry of Domestic Trade and Consumer Affairs (MDTCA) in 1990. Until then, matters pertaining to the welfare of consumers were handled by the Consumer Affairs Division of the Ministry of Trade and Industry set up in 1973. The MDTCA aims to create a healthy environment for domestic trade and to protect consumers from exploitation by unscrupulous businessmen. At the federal level, the Minister appoints the National Advisory Council for Consumer Protection under the Price Control Act 1946 to advise him on consumer issues. At the state and district levels, there are the State Consumer Affairs Council and District Consumer Affairs Council which tackle consumer problems among others. Complex or unresolved consumer problems at the state level are brought to the National Advisory Council.

CONSUMER EDUCATION AND REPRESENTATION

Many consumers are exploited and abused by dishonest profiteering producers and suppliers of goods and services because they are ignorant of their rights as consumers. For others, it is a case of consumer apathy. Consumers would rather have others carry out the collective responsibility while they sit back and reap the benefits. The level of literacy in the country also plays a role in the ability to create consumer awareness. In each country, the struggle is somewhat different. The right market framework does not create itself and the consumer has to be actively involved in pressing for public-spirited rules. Without active consumer participation, only minimal progress can be expected from consumer organisations. Furthermore, for competitive markets to work, consumers must have access to clear information in a form that they can understand. They must be able to know who is offering the service, how much it costs and what they can expect for the price. Consumer education, therefore, is a priority function of consumer organisations.

The electronic media, in particular, provides an effective means for reaching a wide audience. In Malaysia, officials of the Ministry of Domestic Trade and Consumer Affairs participate in consumer talk shows and forums, while in Malta consumers are given the opportunity to air their views on matters related to consumer protection. In the former, consumer education videos are produced and distributed to hospitals, schools, railway stations and airports. In the latter, the Department of Consumer Affairs produces leaflets on consumer rights and obligations and publishes a quarterly educational leaflet called 'Fair Deal'. Talks are delivered in secondary schools and other interested organisations by the Department's Education Officer.

In South Africa, consumer education has been taken a step further with its incorporation in 1995 into the formal syllabus of the subject 'Guidance' taught in primary and secondary schools. A strategy employed by Sierra Leone's Consumer Protection Council is to organise games and sports activities, using these occasions to sensitise people about the organisation and its activities, as well as the government's views on trade and consumer issues. These meetings have helped to create understanding among youths and have increased the organisation's membership. The Consumer Affairs Bureau of Solomon Islands has a consumer information centre that has proved popular with mothers wishing to know where to get cheaper and good quality goods.

Closely related to the need to create awareness is the need for product end users to be involved in the decision-making process on consumer-related issues. Through consumer organisation efforts, consumers are now increasingly represented on governmental and non-governmental decision-making bodies. The case of South Africa is notable in this instance. For decades in South Africa, decisions concerning consumers were taken by authorities without these users participating in the decision-making process. In the present participatory democratic government, the consumer organisation has requested the authorities at all levels to ensure that consumers are properly represented on all bodies where discussions that affect consumer welfare are held.

It is important to remember that consumers are not homogeneous. The process of consulting them is in most cases likely to result in the presentation of different wants and needs. The act of decision-making should take the various desires expressed into consideration and consumers should be provided with a feedback on the factors that influenced decisions made. Another important factor is that consumer consultation can be cost-intensive and this needs to be budgeted for right at the beginning.

REDRESS

Consumers require adequate protection from the excessive and insolent use of power in the public sector, as well as in the free market economy. In general, consumer organisations receive complaints on matters relating to the supply of goods and services, dealing with them directly or referring them to the appropriate public authority. In a number of Commonwealth countries, consumers are protected by common law and redress is sought through the courts. But for many, this in effect means a denial of justice because of the high cost of litigation. In Sierra Leone, the Consumer Protection Council has, therefore, advocated the formation of a consumer court. In South Africa, there exists a Small Claims Court created to assist the ordinary person by resolving matters cheaply and speedily. The court has jurisdiction over credit matters only and claims not exceeding R3000 (about £300). Lawyers are precluded from appearing in this court; litigants appear in person and only natural persons can be plaintiffs.

In Malta, in cases where an amicable settlement is not reached by the Department of Consumer Affairs within 15 working days, the consumer can submit the case to the Consumer Claims Tribunal, which was set up in 1994. The consumer can obtain redress from the tribunal quickly and without incurring any costs. The tribunal is empowered to deal with claims relating to the hire or purchase of goods or services if the value in dispute does not exceed LM 500 (about £300). Consumers may be awarded up to LM 100 (about £60) compensation for distress, anxiety and inconvenience suffered. On the conviction of the offender, the court issues a compensation order in favour of the aggrieved consumer who has suffered pecuniary loss. The maximum amount that can be claimed for such a loss is LM 250 (about £150) and another LM 100 (about £60) for moral damages. In 1995, the Small Claims Tribunal was set up to further simplify the process of consumer redress. At this tribunal, consumers can seek redress by claiming compensation not exceeding LM 100 (£60).

In the UK, the Office of Telecommunications (OFTEL) ensures that telephone companies have good complaints handling systems in place so that if service standards are not met or consumers are badly treated, consumers can get proper redress including compensation in some situations. OFTEL as the watchdog has a statutory role to investigate complaints on behalf of people who are still not satisfied about their telecommunications service, and to request the telephone companies to take remedial action.

VIII. CONSUMER ORGANISATIONS AT WORK

THE 'SPACE' FOR CONSUMER ORGANISATIONS

The following case study is based on the experience of Canada. Canada is a confederation with important powers at the provincial level. Health care, for example, (a top priority among consumer leaders in Canada) comes within the jurisdiction of each province. Trucking and much of transportation is under provincial jurisdiction and internal trade cannot be directed federally. Likewise, there is no national Securities and Exchange Commission in Canada. The result of the distribution of political power is a need for a set of institutions, including consumer institutions, appropriately aligned to meet human needs.

A second major distinction crucial to the understanding of consumer organisation in Canada is the natural monopoly in consumer testing in North America for all those products whose brands and models are marketed internationally. If consumer reports published by the Consumers' Union of the USA do a first-rate job testing automobiles, audio equipment and detergents, there is no market for a Canadian consumer organisation to repeat the tests, and no chance to collect revenue from product tests to use in advocacy work. In Canada, as in other countries, consumer action (advocacy) is hard to finance. The usual 'free-rider problem' applies, where each consumer prefers to let someone else do the work while riding free on the benefit without personally paying anything.

Thirdly, monopolies are significant in Canada. The private sector in Canada has always been about twice as monopolised as is the case in the USA. In addition, the public sector, which is more important, has also led to serious problems with monopoly.

THE HISTORY OF THE CONSUMERS' ASSOCIATION OF CANADA SINCE 1897

Canada, like other countries, made early moves toward the market economy without the institutions required to ensure that exchanges were fair. As early as 1897, a confederation of Canadian women's groups founded the National Council of Women to urge weighing standards and accurate grading of foods and other consumer goods. A breakthrough came in December 1941. Canada had been at war for two years and was facing a crisis with shortages and sharp increases in domestic prices. The Minister of Finance and others called together as many women's organisations as possible to establish a Consumer Advisory Committee in each province and in many cities. Success was immediate, as was the lesson on the effectiveness of collective action.

In early 1947, the Committee was transformed into a coalition that eventually became the Consumers Association of Canada (CAC), a not-for-profit organisation, independent of government and industry. During the 1970s, membership exceeded 150,000. The formation of CAC in 1947 makes it one of the earliest consumer organisations in the world, with only organisations in the USA and Denmark having longer histories.

Some of the early consumer issues in Canada now seem insignificant but they signalled a major change from seller control of the market place. The first victory for CAC came in 1948 when it fought restrictive practices that favoured butter producers and got the ban on margarine lifted. In 1961, consumers in central Canada learnt to their horror that they had been eating meat from animals which were dead before being brought to the meat-packers. The 'dead animal scare' galvanised consumers into action.

Canadians received another shock from thalidomide births in the early 1960s. These birth defects in Canada and in Europe clearly demonstrated the need for public policy. On other fronts, CAC succeeded in getting Canada to create a safe list of food additives, and it helped obtain a Hazardous Products Act (1970). Other components of the market framework include Textile Labelling (1949), Standardised Packaging (1971) and, in some provinces, elements of truth in lending. One of CAC's major successes is Canada's Competition Act which was passed in two stages: covering services in 1976 and merger provisions in 1986.

Canada introduced anti-monopoly provisions in 1889 but the law must have been the laughing stock of monopolists because in a century of its existence, the govern-ment has not won a single contested case. The result is the exceptional degree of monopoly in Canada. CAC was virtually alone at the beginning of its 16-year campaign in calling for a fair and competitive set of laws for billions of market transactions. The new competition framework has worked well and without much 'hands on' administration. This has proved to be a useful lesson. A spectacular failure came in 1974, when a supply restriction system was introduced for milk, eggs, chicken and turkey products. The milk quota alone cost consumers an extra billion dollars annually through high prices.

The 1969 Pharmaceutical Patent arrangement was for a time a success owing much to CAC. The 1969 policy required the second marketer of a patented product to pay a compulsory royalty to the patent holder as a reward for the invention. Yet the policy introduced a measure of market competition in the form of the licensed product. The entry of a second brand set some limit to how high the price could be set by the original monopolist. The policy was assessed in an official inquiry (Eastman Report, 1985) to be ' ... a mechanism to provide socially optimal patent protection ... [a policy] that other countries might well emulate'. Unfortunately, it was important to the multinational drug firms that this working example of an effective policy be snuffed out. In 1987 it was, after what must be the largest lobbying campaign in Canadian history.

A minor gain from CAC's public interest work has been the creation of a Patented Medicine Prices Review board. This is decidedly inferior to the 1969 policy. The Prices Board has been only partially successful on the price front. It issues annual reports showing that very few of the 'new' patented products actually offer much benefit to consumers. 'Breakthrough products' account for fewer than five products per 100 drugs patented. Overall, Canadian consumers lost out decisively as health costs increased by hundreds of million of dollars per year.

Canadian consumers have received major benefits from CAC's half a century of campaigning for freer trade. In the face of ideological polemics and heavy lobbying by special interests, CAC managed to keep its focus on practical issues like health standards, tariff and non-tariff barriers, and monopoly pricing. Some improvements are evident but the restrictive detail in the actual trade agreements severely reduces the potential for them to offer benefits to consumers. This provides a case for strongly supporting the need for consumers to be included as full partners in trade discussions from the very start of negotiations.

FOUR INSTITUTIONS CRUCIAL TO MARKET SUCCESS

Canada has the four crucial institutions needed to ensure that the market operates to improve consumer welfare which are so often assumed in economic theories but which are lamentably absent in practice.

A transparency regime: It is generally known that sellers can take advantage of the lack of information by using ignorance as the basis for discrimination among consumers. It has also been shown that there are conditions under which the market cannot be expected to ensure that quality is delivered. In conditions where a consumer cannot detect the difference in quality, the market fails to offer superior products. The market environment in Canada contains weight and measure laws, truth-in-packaging requirements and other components of the transparency regime. These can be seen in the achievements of the Consumers' Association of Canada listed at the end of this section. The list categorises the achievements in terms of:

- Consumer information
- Market transparency
- Competition measures.

In Canada, it is true that in the financial and environmental sectors, more progress is required. But on the whole, most of the essential transparency provisions are close to the best available practices. The addition of these measures represents a crucial change in the market environment.

Collective consumer search capital: Some institutions which allow consumers to find superior products and services are provided collectively. The origin of the pressure for food and drug regulation or for traffic lights arose in Canada, as elsewhere, from well-recognised scandals or from evident shortcomings of actual selling incidents. The thalidomide case is an example.

Competition policy: In Canada, it has proved to be extremely difficult to establish a policy that prohibits abusive selling practices and encourages competition. CAC was a lone voice in 1969 trying to provide public pressure for a competitive framework. As indicated above, the Act passed in 1976 and 1986 has been a sharp improvement. However, attempts to get trade policies that truly benefit consumers have been less successful. The regional trade agreements (the Canada-US Free Trade Agreement and the North American Free Trade Agreement) actually increased some of the non-tariff barriers to trade.

In the count for the Consumers' Association of Canada (see Table 1), the framework items relating directly or indirectly to competition add up to more than half of the achievements. These are important because it is impossible to fight every fire as it breaks out. It is more effective to change the incentive system so that anti-consumer fires do not take place in the first place. A competition policy is absolutely essential if the consumer is to benefit from liberalised markets.

Collective consumer organisation: The citizen needs the fundamental right to criticise those in power – the rulers and the monopolists – or no progress can be made. This requires certain guarantees on speech and on the right to organise.

WHAT DOES THE CANADIAN EXPERIENCE MEAN FOR OTHER COUNTRIES?

Firstly, it illustrates that there is nothing automatic that causes the 'free market' to create the framework institutions which permit the market to serve consumers. Yet the fundamental structure for fair competition does not require a huge bureaucracy. The Competition Bureau in Canada sets out rules for fair market practices with fewer than 400 administrators. The rules on mergers, for example, are clear enough to be understood in advance most of the time, without hands-on administration. Similarly, the transparency institutions can be constructed without the need for a huge bureaucracy.

Secondly, Canada's experience shows that not every self-proclaimed friend of the market is a friend of consumers. Powerful interests arrange the market institutions to suit their purposes. For example, the lobbyists who arranged for the so-called free market to provide monopoly profits to pharmaceutical firms managed to provide a single firm in Canada with an added bonus of over a billion dollars. Much more money can be made setting up the market institutions to suit one's own interest than can be made producing the real output.

Progress in Canada, as elsewhere, has depended on the existence of public-spirited action groups willing to press for the creation of institutions that reflect the broader interest. This is not routinely to be expected and may indeed need encouragement because of the underlying free-rider problem.

Table 1. Major issues addressed by the Consumers' Association of Canada, 1947–97

Year	Major Issue	Type
1947–48	Prices; Refrigerator safety; Ban on margarine	I F F
1948–50	Seek federal consumer agency; 13,000 members	I T F
1950–53	Remove deception in packaging of bacon	T
1953–56	Restrictive trade practices; advertising	F T
1956–60	Food stamps removed; vitamins	F I
1961–66	Dead animal/food; Consumer Magazine	T F I
1966–69	Federal consumer ministry 1967; grassroots	I T F
1969–70	Drug patent royalty programme: pollution	F T F
1970–71	Hazardous products; health and professions	F I F
1971–74	Publishing with CU; farm quotas; regulation	I F F
1974–76	Competition Act; food prices	F T F
1976–78	Environment, international movement: sales tax	F I T F F
1978–80	Testing labs expanded; food safety/labels	I T
1980–82	Postal monopoly; pesticides	F I T F
1982–84	Telephone rates; electricity	F F
1984–88	Interest rate disclosure. drug lobby trade	T F F
1988–89	Bank fees; health; insurance	I F F F
1989–90	Canada-US Free Trade; end drug patent plan	F F
1990–93	Deregulation consumer ministry downgraded	F I F
1993–94	NAFTA; Magazine ends: information privacy	F I T
1994–95	Information highway; financial sector reform	F T F
1995–96	Health; telephone/cable entry and prices	F F T
1996–97	Service quality, patent medicines, cable; ban	I F F F

I = Information where the consumer group tries to provide information directly to consumers

T = Transparency where the goal is to create institutions to allow for clear decisions among choices

F = Framework policies to provide a framework for competition rather than monopoly or other market forms

Source: Encyclopedia of the Consumer Movement (Brobeck and Mayer, 1997)

IX. PRODUCT TESTING AND QUALITY ASSURANCE

INTRODUCTION

The expansion of the market for consumables, together with the 'luring' advertisement techniques used by manufacturers, marketing organisations and traders makes it increasingly difficult for the consumer always to make the correct choice. It is a known fact that in conditions where a consumer cannot detect the difference in quality, the market fails to reward superior offerings. This is a prevailing situation in much of the new global market place. Therefore, the consumer needs to be provided with unbiased information on the characteristics of the products offered him on the market to enable him make a choice that best meets his particular needs.

COMPARATIVE PRODUCT TESTING

Consumer empowerment can be promoted by making available to consumers the results of laboratory tests. In some cases, they may be subjective assessments made in accordance with methods and criteria judged adequate to provide a meaningful objective comparison of prices, specific performance characteristics and other complementary criteria of the products under review, including likely effects on the environment, safety, etc.

Consumers may also be provided with other relevant information about products of the same kind. This is largely achieved through a comparative product testing programme, which generally consists of the overall evaluation of different products or services of the same kind. It involves the compilation of characteristics, many of which may be non-technical, and may be influenced by prevailing conditions in the social environment, country, region (existing legislation, customs and traditions) or the market under survey. Technical tests should, however, be based on internationally accepted procedures. Typical features investigated about the product are its performance (measure of how it performs its purpose); its convenience and comfort (measure of the interaction between the product and its user); its reliability (the ability of the product to continue to perform its function or work); its durability (how long the product or its component endure); and its safety (assessment of whether the product will is likely to expose its user or bystander to a hazardous situation).

Comparative product testing is cost-intensive, requiring regular and adequate funding. The need to overcome this problem gave rise to the internationalisation of product testing. European consumer organisations do not test the same brand of products but instead have developed a network of information sharing. The Australian Consumer Association tests consumer products for New Zealand. Similar plans have been suggested for Asian countries where India, for example, can carry out laboratory tests for countries in the region which lack such facilities. The International Organisation for Standardisation provides further assistance through its *Guide on Comparative Testing of Consumer Products*. This guide sets out in detail principles which apply to the conduct of comparative testing of products for the information of the consumer.

Products submitted for tests should be sufficiently representative of the variety of products offered on the market for the same purpose. The comparative testing body may deal with a limited selection of products if there are specific aspects of interest to the consumer such as safety or doubtful effectiveness, or it may limit itself to a given price range. Precautions should be taken to ensure that the results obtained are representative of the products on the market. These may include an assessment as to whether a fault is due to poor design or to an exceptional product failure; the checking of results against the manufacturer's specification; the substitution or repair of a sample; the presentation of certain test results individually to manufacturers for comment; and the experience of consumers themselves.

With certain products, such as perishable goods, particular attention should be paid to the trading channels used for the purchase, the condition of sampling, transport and storing before testing in order to ensure the validity and comparability of test results. All characteristics of the product that are relevant to its use by the consumer should, as far as possible, be taken into account. These may include running costs and likely total costs for ownership, safety, health, the effect on the environment, the conservation of natural resources and energy consumption. Attention should also be given to other aspects relevant to product satisfaction like packaging, delivery, installation, instructions for use, guarantees, maintenance costs and servicing, including the availability of spare parts.

The evaluation and presentation of test results should be made in a manner that is technologically sound but in terms that can be easily understood by consumers. In assessing all test results, care must be taken not to emphasise differences between products that are not of practical importance or that are relatively insignificant to consumers. The final comparative test report may suggest a number of best possible purchases. These conclusions should leave the ultimate decision to consumers but may nevertheless stress those products that may represent the best value for money. The Office of Telecommunications presently employs this method in the United Kingdom. The regulatory body successfully persuaded all players in the telecommunications industry to collect comparable information on quality of service measures. This was then made public so that consumers could see which operator was best at what. It has proved to be a good incentive for quality of service improvement.

SAFETY STANDARDS AND ENSURING QUALITY

Closely related to the issue of product testing are the issues of safety and quality. The basic objective in establishing safety standards and ensuring quality is to protect the consumer against avoidable and unreasonable risks. This is particularly important where risks may not be readily apparent to the user, as is the case with toxic hazards. Manufacturers have an important part to play in educating the consumer on the safe handling of their products. Information and instructions should be given where appropriate. How comprehensive and effective these are depends partly on the manufacturer's ability to anticipate likely uses and misuses and their assessment of the associated risks. For the consumer, therefore, the most reliable means of assessing the quality of products are certification marks that denote conformity with standards.

Safety is determined against standards. The process of setting standards should contain clear and complete statements specifying methods for the verification of proper design (for example, type tests and the number of test specimens) and, where appropriate, methods of verification of proper manufacture (for example, acceptance and routine tests) and their compliance criteria. If the standard includes sampling inspection procedures, attention has to be paid to carefully defining how samples are to be taken, sampling plans and the criteria for conformity.

In addition, Commonwealth countries have various forms of standards organisations and in recent times considerable progress has been made through these in preventing goods that are unsafe from reaching the consumer. In Ghana, the Standards Board is the sole body empowered to operate a Certification Mark Scheme. In 1992, a law on product labelling was passed to further protect the consumer. The law makes it an offence for any person to offer for sale, distribute, import or otherwise dispose of pre-packaged food or drugs, unless the food or drug is properly marked or labelled. Information required to be given includes name, ingredients with the amount used in the case of drugs, manufacture and expiry dates, any special storage and handling instructions, directions for use, code marks, country of origin, and the names and addresses of the producers, importers and distributors.

Over the years, Commonwealth countries have come to realise that product inspection is not in itself sufficient to assure quality or, indeed, to eliminate associated problems. Two important developments have taken place as a result. First, many have now committed themselves to various international standards such as the ISO 9000 series (see Chapter II). Quality assurance standards, however, do not by themselves guarantee the commitment of everybody in the organisation to a quality programme, which leads us to the next point. The second important development in the Commonwealth has been the popularisation of the Total Quality Management (TQM) philosophy in individual organisational settings or as part of broader national public sector reform programmes. But, as will be expected, countries that have implemented TQM as a parallel to their national reform programmes have tended to be less successful with both. TQM moves away from the notion of quality as a measure of the final product or service. Instead, it pursues a comprehensive approach to the entire management and production system, involving everyone in the necessary activities that provide for continuous improvement and for achieving sustained high-level quality performance.

Box 9

WHAT IS ISO 9000?

The history of ISO 9000 dates back to the construction of the first nuclear submarines and power stations in the USA in the 1950s. In March 1987 the International Standards for Quality Systems published (ISO 9000–9004). Undoubtedly, the publication of the ISO 9000 series has brought about an international recognition of quality system assessments.

The ISO 9000 is a series of standards for a quality management and assurance system. It sets out the methods by which a management system, incorporating all the activities associated with quality, can be implemented in an organisation to ensure that all the special performance requirements and the needs of the customer are fully met. It applies to the quality management systems used, not the product. It can be applied to almost every manufacturing or service organisation. The ISO 9000 series requires objective evidence at all stages of a process, from material purchase to final delivery to the customer, that work is being carried out to agreed standards.

The ISO 9000 series is a set of five individual, but related, standards. Two of these, ISO 9000 and 9004, are guidelines. The remaining standards, ISO 9001, 9002 and 9003, provide for three levels of quality assurance:

ISO 9001 provides a model for an organisation which is involved in the management or design as well as in producing its own product or service.

ISO 9002 provides an appropriate model for many manufacturing industries producing standard items or service organisation such as retailing outlets providing services.

ISO 9003 is used by organisations whose product is already manufactured and is simply inspected before being supplied

Adapted from: D, Bell, P. McBride and G. Wilson (1997). *Managing Quality.*

In respect of goods other than food and drugs, the labelling information includes the name and nature of the goods, code marks indicating batches, manufacture and expiry dates, an indication of the net content, dimensional mass or volume characteristics, electro-technical or chemical characteristics, etc. All such labelling must be in English, the national language. Goods that are not properly labelled are detained. The law provides for the receipt of petitions within seven days of seizure and for the exportation of the goods within 28 days of detention. Goods seized are disposed of in consultation with the Minister of Trade. Goods other than food and drugs covered under the law include such products as electrical motors, general household electrical appliances and accessories, paints, soaps and poultry feed.

Table 2. Elements in the MS ISO 9001, MS ISO 9002 and MS ISO 9003 series of standards

No.	Element	Elements covered in the Series of Standards		
		MS ISO 9001	MS ISO 9002	MS ISO 9003
1.	Management Responsibility	✓	✓	✓
2.	Quality System	✓	✓	✓
3.	Contract Review	✓	✓	✓
4.	Design Control	✓	–	–
5.	Document and Data Control	✓	✓	✓
6.	Purchasing	✓	✓	–
7.	Control of Customer Supplied Product	✓	✓	✓
8.	Product Identification and Traceability	✓	✓	✓
9.	Process Control	✓	✓	–
10.	Inspection and Testing	✓	✓	✓
11.	Control of Inspection, Measuring and Test Equipment	✓	✓	✓
12.	Inspection and Test Status	✓	✓	✓
13.	Control of Nonconforming Product	✓	✓	✓
14.	Corrective and Preventive Action	✓	✓	✓
15.	Handing, Storage, Packaging, Preservation and Delivery	✓	✓	✓
16.	Control of Quality Records	✓	✓	✓
17.	Internal Quality Audits	✓	✓	✓
18.	Training	✓	✓	✓
19.	Servicing	✓	✓	–
20.	Statistical Techniques	✓	✓	✓

MS = Malaysia Standard

Source: The Civil Service in Malaysia – Towards Excellence Through ISO 9000 (1996).

The Trading Standards Section in Malta administers and enforces the Weights and Measures Ordinance, the Quality Control (Exports, Imports and Local Goods). It tests weighing and measuring equipment, adjusting such equipment where necessary and reporting thereon. Test purchases are carried out and the quantity of goods is checked on the spot in the presence of the seller.

South Africa has compulsory safety specifications for electrical products such as household appliances, power tools, lighting appliances and components thereof, incandescent lamps, television receivers, electrical installation accessories, power cable and cord extension sets, plugs, sockets, adaptors, multiplugs and circuit breakers. These compulsory safety specifications are administered by the South African Bureau of Standards. Compulsory specifications for food products include canned seafood and seafood products, canned meat and meat products. Unknown to many consumers, the South Africa Bureau of Standards has over the years returned a vast number of consignments of unsafe products to their countries of origin before they reached the market place. The chemical and biological safety of most other foodstuffs, as well as food labelling, is mainly governed by the provisions of the Foodstuffs, Cosmetics and Disinfectants Act, 1972. This Act is administered by the Department of Health. Draft regulations on cosmetics are compiled in conjunction with members of the Cosmetics Legislation Advisory Group and are based on guidelines of the European Union before publication for general comment in the *Government Gazette.*

The South African compulsory specifications for motor vehicles and their components are based on regulations issued by the United Nations Economic Commission for Europe. Areas subject to compulsory safety specifications include lighting equipment, mirrors, glass, windscreen wipers, brake performance, controls, crash performance and safety belts. Many South Africans own firearms and the safety of these products are of concern to the authorities. Compulsory specification requires all firearms for civilian use to be proofed before sale and after modification. The requirements are mainly in line with those laid down by the Permanent International Commission for the proofing of portable firearms.

BIBLIOGRAPHY

Australia, Department of Industry Science and Tourism (1997). *Putting Service First – Principles for Developing Service Charters*. Australia, March.

Ayeni, V (ed.) (1992). *Civil Service Transformation for Structural Adjustment*. Lagos: NIM and University of Lagos Press.

Ayeni, V (ed.) (1997). 'Public Administration in Africa', Special Issue, *Politeia* (Pretoria), 16, 2, 129 pp.

Ayeni, V (1997). 'Ombudsman Institutions and Democracy in Africa – A Gender Perspective', *International Ombudsman Journal* (Alberta), Number 1, 1997, pp. 61–76.

Ayeni, V and Lim, A Y (1998). Evaluation of the Work Improvement Teams (WITS) Programme in Botswana – Report of a Commonwealth Secretariat Advisory Mission. London: Commonwealth Secretariat, December.

Barlow, J and Moller, C (1996). *A Complaint is a Gift – Using Customer Feedback as a Strategic Tool*. San Francisco: Berrett-Koehler.

Barrow, A and Scott, C (1992). 'The Citizen's Charter Programme', *The Modern Law Review* (UK), 55, 4, pp. 526–546.

Bell, D, McBride, P and Wilson, G (1997). *Managing Quality*. Oxford: Butterworth & Heinemann.

Bellamy, R and Greenaway, J (1995). 'The New Right Conception of Citizenship and the Citizen's Charter', *Government and Opposition* (UK), 30, 4, pp. 461–491.

Berman J B and Tettey, W J (2001). 'African States, Bureaucratic Culture and Computer Fixes', *Public Administration and Development* (London), 21, 1, February, pp. 1–13.

Blackburn, R (ed.) (1994). *Rights of Citizenship*. London: Mansell.

Blundell, A and Murdock, A (1997). *Managing in the Public Sector*. Oxford: Butterworth–Heinemann.

Canada, Treasury Board (1995). *Quality Services – Guide VII on Service Standards*. Canada: Treasury Board of Canada Secretariat, October.

Cassese, S (ed.) (1999). 'The Citizen and Public Administration', Special Issue, *International Review of Administrative Sciences* (Brussels), 65, 3, September, pp. 307–440.

Cernea, M M (ed.) (1991). *Putting People First – Sociological Variables in Rural Development*. New York: Oxford University Press and The World Bank.

Collins, P and Kaul, M (eds) (1995). 'Government in Transition', Special Issue, *Public Administration and Development* (London), 15, 3, August, pp. 195–343.

Corkery, J et al. (eds) (1998). *Management of Public Service Reform – A Comparative Review of Experiences in the Management of Programmes of the Administrative Arm of Central Government*. Brussels, Amsterdam: IOS Press & Brussels, IIAS.

Corry, Dan, Grand, J and Radcliffe, R (1997). *Public-Private Partnership – A Marriage of Convenience or a Permanent Commitment*. London: Institute of Public Policy Research, March.

Costa, J P and Cananea, G (eds) (1997). *Human Rights and Public Administrations*. Brussels: IIAS.

Farrell, C, Levenson, R and Snape, D (1988). *The Patient's Charter – Past and Future*. London: King's Fund.

Foster, C D and Plowden, F J (1996). *The State Under Stress – Can the Hollow State be Good Government?* Buckingham: Open University Press.

Gabriel, Y and Lang, T (1995). *The Unmanageable Consumer – Contemporary Consumption and its Fragmentation*. London: Sage.

Ghuman, B S (2000). 'Globalisation and Administrative Activity: Towards New Principles and Path for Action', *African Administrative Studies* (Morocco), Number 55, pp. 17–24.

Halachmi, A and Bouckaert, A (eds) (1995). *The Enduring Challenges in Public Management – Surviving and Excellence in a Changing World*. San Francisco: Jossey-Bass Publishers.

Harlow, C (1967). 'Back to Basics – Reinventing Administrative Law', *Public Law* (London), pp. 245–261.

Harris, M and Partington, M (eds) (1999). *Administrative Justice in the 21st Century*. Oxford: Hart.

Heeks, R (ed.) (2001). *Reinventing Government in the Information Age – International Practice in IT-enabled Public Sector Reform*. London & New York: Routledge.

Holmes, S and Sunstein, C R (1999). *The Costs of Rights – Why Liberty Depends on Taxes*. New York: W W Norton & Co.

Holzer, M and Callahan, K (1998). *Government at Work – Best Practices and Model Programs*. London: Sage.

Hood, C and Scott, C (1996). 'Bureaucratic Regulation and New Public Management in the United Kingdom' – "Mirror Image Developments"?' *Journal of Law and Society* (UK), 23, 3, pp. 321–345.

Hood, C et al. (1999). *Regulation inside Government – Waste Watchers, Quality Police and Sleaze-Busters*. Oxford: Oxford University Press.

John, R (ed.) (1994). *The Consumer Revolution – Redressing the Balance*. London: Hodder & Stoughton.

Kaul, M (1995). *From Problem to Solution – Commonwealth Strategies for Reform*. London: Commonwealth Secretariat.

Kaul, M (1998). *Introducing New Approaches – Improved Public Service Delivery*. London: Commonwealth Secretariat.

Lewis, N and Birkinshaw, P (1993). *When Citizens Complain – Reforming Justice and Administration*. Buckingham: Open University Press.

Loffler, E (2001). 'Quality Awards as a Public Sector Benchmarking Concept in OECD Member Countries – Some Guidelines for Quality Award Organizers', *Public Administration and Development* (London), 21, 1, February, pp. 27–40.

Malaysia, Government of (1996). *The Civil Service of Malaysia – Towards Excellence Through ISO 9000*. Kuala Lumpur: MAMPU.

McKevitt, D and Lawton, A (eds (1994). *Public Sector Management – Theory, Critique and Practice*. London: Sage and Open University.

McLagan, P and Nel, C (1995). *The Age of Participation – New Governance for the Workplace and the World*. South Africa: Knowledge Resources.

Myers, R and Lacey, R (1996). 'Consumer Satisfaction, Performance and Accountability in the Public Sector', *International Review of Administrative Sciences* (Brussels), 62, 3, September, pp. 331–350.

Oliver, D (1994). 'Law, Politics and Accountability – The Search for a New Equilibrium', *Public Law* (London), pp. 238–253.

Oliver, M and Barnes, C (1998). *Disabled People and Social Policy – From Exclusion to Inclusion*. London: Longman.

Osborne, D and Garbler, T (1993). *Reinventing Government – How the Entrepreneurial Spirit is Transforming the Public Sector*. New York: New York, Penguin.

Peters, T and Waterman, R. H. (1995). *In Search of Excellence – Lessons from America's Best-Run Companies*. London: Harper Collins Business.

Politt, C and Bouckaert, G (2000). *Public Management Reform – A Comparative Perspective*. Oxford: Oxford University Press.

Prokopenko, J (1987). *Productivity Management – A Practical Handbook*. Geneva: International Labour Office.

Richardson, A (1983). *Participation*. London: Routledge & Kegan Paul.

Robinson, M and White, G (eds) (1998). *The Democratic Developmental State – Political and Institutional Design*. Oxford: Oxford University Press.

Seely, A and Jenkins, P (1996). *The Citizen's Charter*, Research Paper 95/66. London: House of Commons Library, May.

UNDP (2000). *Human Development Report, 2000*. New York: Oxford University Press.

United Kingdom, Cabinet Office (1991). *The Citizen's Charter – Raising the Standards*. London: HMSO, July.

Western Australia, Ministry of the Premier and Cabinet (1995). *Developing Customer Service Charters – A Practical Guide*. Perth, Australia.

Willcocks, L and Harrow, J (eds) (1992). *Rediscovering Public Services Management*. London & New York: McGraw-Hill.

Willett, C (ed.) (1996). *Public Sector Reform and the Citizen's Charter*. London: Blackstone Press.

Wilson, J (ed.) (1995). *Managing Public Services – Dealing with Dogma*. London: Hodder & Stoughton.

World Bank (1997). *The State in a Changing World – World Development Report, 1997*. New York: Oxford University Press.

World Bank (2000). *Entering the 21st Century – World Development Report, 1999/2000*. New York: Oxford University Press.

APPENDIX 1: EXCERPTS FROM THE CHARTER FOR THE PUBLIC SERVICE IN AFRICA

Adopted by the 3rd Biennial Pan-African Conference of Ministers of Civil Service, Windhoek, Namibia, 5 February 2001

PART III – RULES GOVERNING RELATIONS BETWEEN THE PUBLIC SERVICE AND THE USERS

The public service shall serve users in accordance with the following criteria: proximity and accessibility of services; participation, consultation and mediation; quality, effectiveness and efficiency; evaluation of services; transparency and information; speed and responsiveness; reliability and confidentiality of information.

Article 8: Proximity and accessibility of services

The public service shall be organized along functional and decentralized lines designed to bring public management closer to the people and provide them with appropriate and accessible basic services.

Physical proximity and accessibility can be achieved by the application of appropriate information and communication technologies (E-Governance).

Article 9: Participation, consultation and mediation

It shall be the responsibility of the administration to ensure that the mechanisms of participation and consultation involving civil society and other stakeholders are effectively put in place through consultative forums or advisory bodies.

When provision is made in the texts for consultation, the public service may not introduce in its definitive texts, any provision that shall not have been submitted before hand to the relevant advisory body for its opinion.

To avoid conflict of interest no individual who has a direct or indirect vested private interest in the subject matter of any consultation may be a member of an advisory body or take part in its deliberations.

It shall be the responsibility of the public service to put in place a system of mediation through an institution that has sufficient moral and social authority that enables users as well as public service employees themselves to have means of redress other than administrative and/or legal remedies. The mandate of this institution would thus be to ensure that the rights of users and public service employees are upheld for the benefit of all parties concerned.

Article 10: Quality, effectiveness and efficiency

The public service shall ensure that the highest quality and the most effective and efficient services are provided by making optimal use of the resources at its disposal. It shall also take into account the resources and means that users have available to them to benefit from public services.

The public service shall make the necessary adjustments to the way in which its services are organized and operated, in order to respond, on a sustainable basis, to changing needs and the demands of the public at large. These adjustments must lead to better service delivery and must be informed by best practices in the application of the information and communication technologies.

Article 11: Evaluation of services

The evaluation of the effectiveness and productivity of services shall be based on objectives and programmes of activities defined beforehand, accompanied by performance indicators and criteria.

To this end, evaluation mechanisms shall be established in the public service to carry out periodic evaluations of the services offered to the public.

The results of these evaluations shall be disseminated, together with the publication of the annual reports.

Article 12: Transparency and information

Administrative decisions shall always be taken in accordance with transparent, simple and understandable procedures, while ensuring accountability.

All administrative units shall make available all the necessary information on acts and procedures in their respective domains, as wall as the information required to assess their management, with a view to enabling those interested to have full access.

The administration shall inform the person concerned of any decision taken concerning him/her, indicating the reasons for such decision and stating, where necessary, the legal remedies open to him/her, should he/she decide to challenge the decision.

The administration shall establish or strengthen reception and information units for users in order to assist them in gaining access to services and in recording their views, suggestions or complaints.

Article 13: Speed and responsiveness

The public service shall determine and respect deadlines in the delivery of its services.

These deadlines must be established by law and regulations and evidence of unusually long delays, may make the administration liable to legal action.

Failure by the public service to take action upon the expiration of a deadline as stipulated in the law shall be construed as tacit acceptance, unless otherwise expressly provided by the law or regulations.

Article 14: Reliability and confidentiality of information concerning citizens

Personal information or information that helps to identify, in any manner whatsoever, directly or indirectly, the individuals concerned, may not be subject to processing, including computerized processing, in a manner that would violate personal privacy, individual freedoms or human rights.

Any person who can prove his/her identity shall have the right to be informed about any personal information concerning him/her, and to challenge and have such information corrected, if need be. He/she shall also be informed of the use to which such information is put, including in computerized information.

With the exception of administrative departments such as the police and the judiciary, which may be authorized by law to maintain automated personal data files, no files shall contain information on the private life, views, health or individuals, or on any other type of information that may violate the privacy of individuals, without the express authorization of the individuals concerned. Departments must however take cognizance of the complexity of privacy and disclosure in the event of an individual, where a balance has to be found between privacy and public interest (i.e. HIV/AIDS).

APPENDIX 2: SAMPLE SERVICE CHARTER (NHS, United Kingdom)

I. NATIONAL CITIZEN'S CHARTER FRAMEWORK

According to this, NHS patients are entitled to the following rights:

- Good quality care;

- Clear information about the options available for their care or treatment and continuing information about how each case is developing;

- Involvement, as far as is practical, in their own care and treatment;

- Choice of GP, including the opportunity to change easily;

- Control, with a right to give or withhold consent to medical treatment;

- Freedom, with a right to decide whether or not to participate in medical research and student training;

- Respect at all times for privacy, dignity, religious and cultural beliefs;

- Consideration for relatives and friends visiting on enquiring after patients;

- Ability to comment on the care they have received, and to make a formal complaint when they wish;

- Access, with safeguards, to information held about them;

- Satisfaction if these standards are not achieved.

II. LOCAL ADAPTATION OF THE NATIONAL FRAMEWORK: PRACTICE CHARTER OF THE KING EDWARDS MEDICAL CENTRE, LONDON

We are pleased that you are registered as a patient with this practice. We are committed to giving you the best possible service. The best way to achieve this by working in partnership with us.

Help us to help you

We will:

- Greet you in a friendly welcoming manner.

- Treat you as a partner in the care and attention you receive.

- Treat you as an individual and give you courtesy and respect at all times. (Likewise, we would ask you to show the same consideration to the doctors and all the members of our staff.)

- Following discussion, provide you with the most appropriate care and treatment given by our team who are suitably qualified.

- Give you full information about the services we offer and in particular about anything which directly affects your health and care.

- Give you access to your health records, subject to any limitation in the law.

- Advise you and inform you of:
  - Steps you can take to promote good health and to avoid illness
  - Self-help for minor ailments where reference to a doctor is not necessary.

We ask you to:

- Ask us if you don't understand or are unsure about anything to do with your treatment.

- Keep us informed if you change your name, move house, or change your telephone number.

- Help us by asking for visits when the surgery is closed only when you truly need immediate attention.

- Request a home visit only if you are too ill to come to the surgery. If in doubt, please speak to the doctor first.

- Request a home visit before 10.00 am if possible.

- Make a separate appointment and tell us as soon as possible if you can't make it.

- Be ready to give us full information about past illnesses, medication, hospital admissions and anything else that is relevant.

- Ensure you come to a new patient check, if you are a new patient.

- Tell us if we fail to meet these standards so that we can put things rights.

Our Standards:

- You will be able to consult with a Doctor or an appropriate member of our Primary Health Care Team, Practice Nurse, Health Visitor, Midwife, Counsellor or District Nurse
  - Urgent cases and all young children – the same day
  - Non-urgent cases – within 48 hours

- Time waiting to see a doctor or member of the Primary Health Care Team will be no more than 20 minutes unless there are exceptional circumstances of which you would be made aware.

- Home visits:
  - Routine – as soon as possible after morning surgery if requested by 10.00am
  - Urgent – as soon as possible

- Repeat prescriptions (computer) – if a doctor has agreed to give a repeat prescription, please allow at least two working days' notice. (Telephone requests for repeat prescriptions are dangerous and can therefore only be accepted under exceptional circumstances.)

- Written requests for repeat prescriptions may be sent by post, enclosing a stamped addressed envelope, or brought in and collected in person.

- Out of hours Emergency Service – please telephone only if the problem is urgent when the surgery is closed.

- Telephone access to the doctor – the best time to speak to a doctor is between 10.30 and 11.00 am and between 3.45 and 4.00 pm.

- Premises – we will maintain our premises in first class condition in order to provide the necessary care including access for disabled patients.

- Test results – appointment with a doctor or nurse will be made for you to discuss your test results. Please ring after 2.00 pm to ask for results.

- Ethnic Minorities – we respect cultural differences.

- Lady doctor – we do have a lady doctor but she may not be available all the time.

Source: Respective Documents, Citizens Charter Trust, Cabinet Office, London, September 1996.